Ferrets

VICKIE McKIMMEY

Ferrets

Project Team
Editor: Mary E. Grangeia
Copy Editor: Stephanie Fornino
Interior Design: Leah Lococo Ltd. and Stephanie Krautheim
Design Layout: Stephanie KrautheimFirst published in
Cover Design: Angela Stanford

United Kingdom Editorial Team
Hannah Turner
Nicola Parker

First published in the United Kingdom in 2008 by
Interpet Publishing
Vincent Lane
Dorking
Surrey
RH4 3YX

ISBN 978 1 84286 189 9

Printed and bound in China.

This book has been published with the intent to provide accurate and authoritative information in regard to the subject matter within. While every reasonable precaution has been taken in preparation of this book, the author and publisher expressly disclaim responsibility for any errors, omissions, or adverse effects arising from the use or application of the information contained herein. The techniques and suggestions are used at the reader's discretion and are not to be considered a substitute for veterinary care. If you suspect a medical problem consult your veterinarian.

INTERPET
PUBLISHING

www.interpet.co.uk

Table of Contents

Chapter 1

Why I Adore My
Ferret

Delightful and entertaining pets, ferrets are eager, rambunctious, and tireless souls. If you are looking for an interactive companion pet who has all the best qualities of a cat and dog rolled into one, then a ferret might be the right choice for you. Aside from their amusing antics and intelligent nature, ferrets are quite independent, although they thrive on human companionship and can be very social.

Be sure that a ferret is the kind of companion pet you really want, though. Owning a ferret is not the same as owning a dog or cat. A ferret's curiosity, playfulness, and energy can be charming, but also can make him tough to keep up with at times. Ferret-proofing your house is necessary for both your pet's sake and your own. And while most devoted ferret fans don't find their musky scent (which can be minimised with bathing and taking other steps) objectionable, ferrets do have their own very special smell. Make sure that you know what to expect before bringing this lovable creature into your home as part of the family. Find someone in your area who owns a ferret or two, plan a visit, and see just what it's like living with

them before making the long-term commitment yourself.

Natural History

Domestic ferrets, *Mustela furo* (sometimes called *Mustela putorius furo*), are not wild animals. They have been domesticated for a long time, perhaps 2,000 to 3,000 years. Some ferret remains have dated back to 1500 BC, and it is thought that the Egyptians and Greeks kept them as pets.

Generally believed to be descended from the European polecat, domestic ferrets were originally used as hunting animals to catch rabbits and rodents. They weren't supposed to kill the prey, just chase them out of their holes so that farmers and hunters could kill them.

Ferrets are cousins of weasels and otters. (Other relatives include minks, ermines, stoats, badgers, black-footed ferrets, polecats, and fishers.) Although many people mistake them for members of the rodent family, they are carnivorous mammals, and as such, cannot digest vegetables and fruits very well. Not equipped to survive for very long on their own, escaped ferrets would suffer from dehydration, starvation, and exposure, and usually couldn't survive more than a few days unless someone took them in. Unlike cats and dogs, they aren't even large enough to push over rubbish bins to scavenge for food.

Most of the misconceptions regarding domestic ferrets probably come from mistaking them for their wild cousins. It's

Believed to be descended from the European polecat, domestic ferrets were originally used as hunting animals to catch rabbits and rodents.

What Is a Ferret?

Domestic ferrets are small, furry mammals whose average size ranges from 1 to 5 pounds (0.5 to 2.3 kg) at maturity. The ferret is the domesticated member of the order carnivore, family Mustelidae, and genus *Mustela furo*.

Physical Characteristics

As a species, ferrets have numerous anatomical features that suited their ancestral lifestyle well, the most outstanding being strength and flexibility. Perfect for burrowing, or ferreting, the basic shape of the head is triangular, broad between the ears and tapered toward the muzzle in an elliptical shape. Ferrets have comparatively large ears that can hear high-frequency sound (good for locating mice). They have a large nose with an excellent sense of smell. Their long neck allows them to carry large prey without getting it in the way of their front legs. Their five-toed feet

very difficult to tell a polecat or a mink from a domestic ferret when all you've seen is a flash of fur disappearing into a burrow, and polecats and minks are quite common in the less-developed areas of Europe and North America. Because of their similar names, domestic ferrets also have been confused with their cousins, the North American black-footed ferret, *Mustela nigripes*. Black-footed ferrets (BFFs) are wild, remote relatives of the domestic ferret, and despite similar appearances, are not very closely related to them. In fact, they are an endangered species—the only BFFs known to exist are now in zoos or in breeding re-release programmes.

Friendly and intelligent, ferrets will delight you with their silly antics and lively personalities.

The Descenting Myth

Just because your ferret has been descented doesn't mean that he won't have an odour. They have a slightly musky odour, even in the cleanest of situations. No matter how fastidious you may be about hygiene and cage maintenance, you can never completely eliminate your pet's unique odour.

You can use an odour-eliminating spray on bedding, sleep sacks, blankets, and litter boxes—just be sure that it's safe for ferrets. Also, keeping the cage clean and washing bedding at least once a week will help to reduce odour.

and hands offer them exceptional grasping ability, enabling them to easily manipulate objects. (Their thumb is almost opposable!) Mobile shoulders provide for a wide range of motion, which makes ferrets extremely flexible. A springy, flexible rib cage and spine also allow them to do a U-turn in a

Life Span

Ferrets have an average life span of six to nine years, with some living ten years or longer. Some records have even shown that ferrets have lived as long as 15 years, but this is extremely rare. They are considered middle-aged at three to four years of age and seniors at age five. To ensure your pet's longevity, basic daily care should be adjusted to your pet's changing needs during each life phase.

space not quite twice their own diameter. Their back can be stretched long for running in holes or hunched up to conserve energy when above ground. Short legs allow them to move very quickly through extremely narrow passages.

A healthy domestic ferret should exhibit a firm, solid feel to the touch, not flabbiness, which would indicate fat not muscle. He also should present an overall symmetry of body. Both sides, left and right, should be even in length, width, and bulk. A ferret in top condition will have a thick, glossy coat whether it is a summer or winter coat. The winter coat should be long, luxurious, and soft to the touch. The summer coat will have little undercoat but also should be soft and silky.

Colours and Patterns

There is only one "breed" of ferret, but they come in many colours and patterns. Ferrets often change colours with the seasons, becoming lighter in the winter than in the summer, and many of them lighten as they age, too. The various ferret organisations may organise different colours and patterns, but unless you're planning to enter your ferret in a show, the exact colour isn't particularly important.

Although there are many varieties, the basic colours include:

Albino: The albino has a white coat with red eyes and a pink nose.

Black: The black has a black coat with black eyes and a black nose.

Black Sable: The black sable has a blackish-brown coat with black eyes and a black nose.

Champagne: The champagne has a diluted chocolate or tan coat with burgundy or brown eyes and a pink or beige nose.

Chocolate: The chocolate has a warm milk-chocolate brown coat with

Many colour varieties of ferret are bred today. Sable is the most common and true cinnamon is the most rare; this is a sable roan mitt.

brown eyes and a light brown or pink nose.

Cinnamon: The true cinnamon has a rich light reddish brown coat with light to dark burgundy eyes and a brick coloured nose.

Dark-Eyed White: The dark-eyed white (sometimes called a black-eyed white) has a white coat with burgundy eyes and a pink nose.

Sable: The sable has a warm dark-brown coat with brown or black eyes and a brown nose.

The basic patterns include:

Blaze: The blaze can be any coat colour except white and has a wide white stripe on the head with ruby to brown eyes, a pink nose, white feet, and a white bib.

Mitt: The mitt can be any coat colour except white and has white feet and a white bib.

Mutt: The mutt can be any coat colour except white and has mismatched roaning, dots, spots, and patterns.

Panda: The panda can be any coat colour except white and has a full white head with burgundy or ruby

eyes, a pink nose, and white feet or legs.

Point: The point can be any coat colour except white and has a lighter body colour with darker legs and tail colour and a V-shaped mask.

Roan: The roan can be any coat colour and has an even mixture of white to colour hair.

Solid: The solid has the appearance of a solid colour from head to tail with a T-bar mask.

Standard: The standard has a lighter body colour than the legs and tail, but not as dramatic as the point, with a full bandit-style mask.

Striped/Patterned: The striped or patterned is a dark-eyed white with a darker-coloured stripe down the back or a light concentration of coloured hairs over the body.

Temperament and Personality

Ferrets are friendly, smart, funny, and loving, and they make excellent pets. If you've never met one before, the easiest way to think of them is somewhere between cats and dogs in personality. Like cats, ferrets are small, quiet, and easy to care for. Like dogs, they enjoy being with people. They can only see reasonably well, but they have excellent senses of hearing and smell. Some are cuddly, others more independent; they vary a lot in temperament, just like other pets and humans.

Ferrets are a lot of fun. They are very playful with each other and with people, and they don't lose much of

What's in a Name?

The name "ferret" comes from the Latin word *furo*, meaning "thief," and what an appropriate name it is. The ferret operates on the assumption that if he sees something he wants, it should be his, no matter what.

Natural Behaviours

Generally, ferrets have few true temperament problems. Often, however, people perceive some of their instinctual behaviours as "problem behaviours." These situations require patience and dedication on the part of the owner, who needs to work through them before they get out of control and develop into circumstances that cannot be lived with. As frustrating and unusual as you'll find some of these behaviours, remember that they are the very traits that early ferret owners found most attractive. The following is a list of common ferret behaviours and their original purposes. Keep in mind that very few other species have retained so much of their original qualities throughout the centuries.

Biting: Necessary for killing prey (rodents).

Digging: Necessary for burrowing to search out and destroy prey.

Tunnelling: Ability to "ferret" into almost any tight space (same as above).

Cunning and sly behaviour: Necessary to be a formidable adversary for savvy prey.

Marking: The fact that ferrets are not necessarily creatures of habit when it comes to their toilet practices is because, in nature, they put their scent over a wide area to act as a deterrent for rodent populations in granaries.

FAMILY-FRIENDLY TIP

Ferrets and Kids

Do ferrets make good pets for children? Yes! Ferrets combine the best features of dogs and cats with some unique features of their own. Like cats, ferrets are small, quiet, and easy to care for. Like dogs, they are affectionate, playful, and enjoy human interaction. Their mischievous and playful nature, retained well into old age, makes them entertaining companions that love the attention and company of their humans.

However, because kids can be excitable and frenetic at times, be sure that your ferret has settled into family life before allowing them to interact with him. Also, as with all pets, teach kids that ferrets are living, breathing, fragile creatures that must be handled with care. It is never acceptable to scare or hurt a pet. It goes without saying that children always should be supervised when visiting with animals.

because they are inquisitive and remarkably determined—which is part of their charm — they can get into plenty of trouble, so be prepared!

Social animals, ferrets do come to know and love their keepers, although it may take a while for some individuals to fully bond. They can be trained to use a litter box and to do tricks, and most of them love to go places with you, whether riding on a shoulder or in a bag. They sleep a lot, and they don't particularly mind staying in small places temporarily (a cage or a shoulder bag, for instance), although they need to run around and play outside of their enclosures for at least several hours a day.

A single ferret won't be terribly lonely, although the fun of watching two or three playing together is easily worth the small amount   of extra trouble. Barring accidents, ferrets will typically live six to nine years, so owning one is a long-term commitment. They have many good points as pets, but there are some negatives as well. Like kittens and puppies, they require a lot of care and training at first. They're higher maintenance than

that playfulness as they get older. They can be entertaining companions with proper socialisation. More intelligent than cats and dogs, they demonstrate this trait in their constant curiosity and mischievous behaviour. However,

Ferrets typically live six to nine years, so owning one is a long-term commitment.

cats; they'll take more of your time and attention. Ferrets have their own distinct scent, which bothers some people, and many of them aren't quite as good about litter trays as cats are. Although most ferrets get along reasonably well with cats and dogs, it's not guaranteed, so if you have large, aggressive pets (particularly dog breeds commonly used for hunting), keep that in mind. Likewise, small children and ferrets are very excitable, and the combination might be too much.

Finally, the importance of ferret-proofing must be emphasised. Ferrets are less destructive than cats, but they love to get into everything. So if you let them roam free, you'll need to make sure that they can't hurt themselves or your possessions. They love to steal small (and not so small!) objects and stash them under chairs and behind furniture. They like to chew on spongy, springy things, so keep them out of reach or your pet could swallow bits, which are choking hazards and could cause intestinal impaction. Ferrets will crawl into accessible boxes, bags, and rubbish bins and houseplants within reach are liable to lose all their dirt to joyful digging. Many ferrets tend to scratch and dig at the carpet. Naturally, these traits vary from one ferret to another, but they're all pretty common. If you're not willing to take the necessary time to protect your property and your pet, a ferret may not be the pet for you.

Male vs. Female

As with people, a ferret's personality is more important than his colour or gender. There's no consistent personality difference between males and females once they are neutered. Males (called hobs) and females (called jills) are slightly different in size. Males are generally considerably larger, about 18 inches (46 cm) and 3 to 5 pounds (1.4 to 2.3 kg) compared to about 15 inches (38 cm) and 0.75 to 2.5 pounds (0.3 to 1.3 kg) for females. The head of the male will be broader than that of the female.

If you get ferrets from a pet shop, they are already neutered. If you get one from a breeder who hasn't offered this service, you will need to alter him or her (unless, of course, you're specifically planning to breed your pets). It will be almost impossible to keep a male ferret who has not been descented and neutered as an

The Expert Knows

This Business of Ferrets

A male is called a hob, a female is called a jill, and a baby ferret is a kit. The most commonly accepted phrase for a group is "a business of ferrets." If you can't tell whether you have a male or female, it's probably a female. Look on the belly of the ferret, about halfway between the tail and the bottom of the rib cage. If you see what looks like a belly button, your ferret is a male—and it's not a belly button. Otherwise, just look for a second opening, perhaps with a tiny flap of skin. If you see that, your ferret is a female. To double-check, look at a once-used litter tray. Ferrets usually urinate and defecate in one "sitting," and because of the anatomy described here, males leave puddles a few inches (cm) in front of their piles, while females leave puddles right on top.

indoor pet. Aside from the behaviour problems that will definitely occur in a fully fertile male, the musky odour can be overwhelming. A female who has not been spayed possibly may be less smelly, but you will have the problem of her oestrus (heat) cycles, which actually can lead to aplastic anaemia and death if she is not spayed or bred.

Age Differences

Young ferrets, or kits, are more lively and entertaining than older ferrets. Of course, even adult ferrets still can be likened to young kittens in their playful antics at times.

It takes considerable time and effort to train a young kit. He'll need constant attention regarding housetraining and litter box training, and you will have to be firm regarding rowdy play. A kit who is allowed to bite and nip during play will likely grow up to be an adult who may be hard to handle.

An adult ferret is well past all the training stages and a youngster's mischievousness. He tends to be a bit calmer, and because he has learned to accept you as part of *his* family, you'll share years of fun and adventure together.

More Than One?

Ferrets don't need other ferrets to be happy. One ferret certainly can be happy if given enough toys and social stimulation. But if you won't be around much, two or more will keep each other company. Because they are social creatures, a ferret probably will appreciate having a "partner in crime." They'll also be more fun, although they'll require a bit more responsibility.

You can keep one ferret at first so that you can get to know each other and have a chance to bond. There's some advantage to only having to train one animal at a time, too. If you decide you want to keep more, you can always get another later. If you're going to get several ferrets, I'd suggest waiting at least a month, although it's certainly not necessary.

Individuals usually will get along fine, and there's generally no problem mixing neutered ferrets of either gender in any combination. However, if you adopt adult male ferrets, make certain that they both have been neutered. An adult male may become so territorial that he may kill any other ferret who shares his cage. You don't have to choose littermates or ferrets

The more your ferret gets to know and interact with you and other pets, the faster he'll become a happy, well-adjusted member of your family.

who have been caged together either. After a brief socialisation time, the average ferret quickly will adapt to having a strange ferret roommate, and soon you'll find them snoozing together in their hammock or playing together and sharing their toys.

Ownership Responsibilities

As a responsible pet owner, you must ensure the best possible life for your ferret. He is a living, breathing, social creature who wants and needs to be accepted fully into the heart and home of his new family. This includes a good deal of time spent outside the cage (several hours a day), which should be large, spacious, and tidy, and placed in an active part of the household so as to make him feel like a member of your family.

Just as you would for any other pet, you must provide for your ferret's every comfort, in addition to providing the basic daily care necessary to keep him clean, healthy, and happy. Unfortunately, a ferret's life span is not as long as that of a dog or cat, but these adorable creatures will add so much to your life that they are well worth the effort it takes to keep them around for as long as possible.

Owning any pet is a serious long-term commitment, but more so because a ferret is not the usual family pet. People who own ferrets are quick to tell you that they're not for everyone, although they are the perfect choice for the right person. Once you've made the decision to share your home with a ferret or two, prepare yourself for a life filled with joy, laughter, and the occasional frustration.

Ferret Resources

Ferrets are one of the most popular interactive companion pets and are ranked third behind dogs and cats. They are kept by people from all walks of life, both young and old alike.

If you want to learn more about your ferret or have any questions regarding his care, the British Ferret Club (BFC) can direct you to numerous resources, including the most up-to-date information on veterinarians, medical procedures, breeding, ferret clubs, and showing, as well as how to protect the species. You can contact them at:

The British Ferret Club
www.britishferretclub.co.uk

The British Ferret Club

The British Ferret Club was established in 2000 with the intention of bringing together people who regard ferrets with respect and affection.

The Club was originally formed to raise the profile of ferrets and to encourage the best practice in the keeping of ferrets. This includes ferret welfare, care, nutrition and the breeding of working ferrets and pet ferrets.

The National Ferret Welfare Society

The National Ferret Welfare Society (NFWS) was formed in 1986 from the remnants of an earlier society and attempts to bring together those interested in improving the lives of ferrets, whether workers or pets, from all parts of the United Kingdom and the rest of the world.

The aim of the Society is to educate members in ferret care and general husbandry and to promote their correct and most effective use in vermin control.

Why I Adore My Ferret

Chapter 2

The Stuff of Everyday Life

Bringing a pet into your life requires a long-term commitment, and because your ferret will be with you for at least six to ten years, you should have everything he'll need to feel safe and comfortable in his new home. Your responsibility to keep him happy and healthy will take some effort on your part, but the rewards far outweigh the work involved.

To properly care for your ferret, you need certain basic supplies. You have to provide him with a large, roomy cage where he can spend his time when he's not with you. It should be a pleasant place for him, filled with interesting toys, cosy bedding, food and water, and a litter box.

A complete list of essentials includes the following:

- cage (made specifically for ferrets)
- food bowls, water bowls, and water bottles
- litter box and ferret-friendly litter
- bedding, ferret sleep sacks, and hammocks
- safe, appropriate ferret toys and tubes
- ferret harness and lead
- grooming supplies (ferret shampoo, brush, nail clippers, etc.)
- pet carrier

An Appropriate Cage

Unlike cats and dogs, ferrets simply cannot be given free run of the house; it is too dangerous. An appropriate cage is an absolute must. (I usually advise folks not to bring a new ferret home until they have the cage and all the supplies for it.) When it comes to safety and comfort, there are some do's and don'ts regarding proper cages. If you follow these guidelines, you will save money, time, and heartache in the long run.

Cage Do's

- Ferrets should be housed in a sturdy wire cage (for good ventilation).
- The enclosure should be large enough to allow your ferret ample room to move around. It should be at least 30 to 36 inches (76 to 91 cm) long, 18 to 24 inches (46 to 61 cm) wide, and a minimum of 20 inches

Your ferret's cage should be a roomy, pleasant place for him, filled with interesting toys, cosy bedding, food and water, and a litter box.

(51 cm) high. Some rabbit cages are suitable and were often used in years past. Today, there is a wide variety of good cages on the market.

- The cage should have plenty of available floor space. Ferrets are not happy in cages with steep ramps and small ledges. They are ground-dwelling animals who like to burrow into tunnels to sleep. They are not tree climbers like cats.

- The cage door should have an opening big enough for a litter tray to fit through for ease of cleaning and regular maintenance.

- The cage should have a strong latch and be escape-proof. If it is not, your ferret will try to squeeze through any open space. If he tries to get out and gets stuck, the results could be fatal. Be careful with spring latches.

- Use a washable piece of carpet or something just as soft for the cage floor. Ferret paws were not designed for bare wire floors.

- Make sure that the cage has a distinct sleeping, feeding, and toilet areas. The litter box should be kept at a distance from the sleeping and eating areas. Secure it to one corner of the cage.

- Keep the cage in a cool, shaded, dry area away from drafts and direct sunlight. Ferrets have a limited number of sweat glands and are most comfortable in temperatures of 60° to 70°F (15.6° to 21.1°C). They cannot tolerate temperatures above 80°F (26.7°C) or high humidity. If your ferret becomes overheated,

Solid or Wire?

When it comes to cage floors, the type you select is pretty much a matter of your personal preference rather than that of your ferret's. Either choice is appropriate. Solid cage floors will need to be tidied up more often because food, litter, and hair will accumulate if not removed. Wire cage floors allow these items to fall into a catch tray that can be lined with newspaper for easy cleaning. However, they should be of wire mesh no larger than 0.5 x 0.5 inches (1.3 x 1.3 cm). Vinyl-coated wire will make it easier on your ferret's feet. With both choices, you should provide a floor covering. Fabric, vinyl tiles, and carpet remnants work best.

he could die of heatstroke within minutes.

- Your ferret requires time out of his cage. Give him at least two hours (and more is better) of exercise and interaction with you on a daily basis.

- Regular weekly cage maintenance is a must; your ferret's home should be kept as clean as possible. Use a nontoxic disinfectant made for cleaning cages to help to destroy germs.

- Put your ferret back in his cage when he's tired. Also, cage him when you are not at home, during parties, when guests or strangers are coming and going, and during any other unique or unfamiliar occasion to prevent accidents.
- Make sure that your ageing ferret can get in and out of his cage easily. Provide ramps if necessary.

If you cannot find an appropriate cage, the British Ferret Club (BFC) can direct you to some resources that will help you find one to fit your needs.

Cage Don'ts

- Don't use small cages as ferret housing.
- Don't use cages with small ledges and steep ramps. Ferrets require plenty of floor space in their enclosures.
- Don't use painted or pressure-treated woods or metals containing toxins such as zinc or lead as housing materials.
- Don't use an aquarium as an enclosure. They are unsanitary and unhealthy places to keep ferrets. The ventilation is terrible, and the damp and stale air causes respiratory problems. Aquariums are for fish, not ferrets.
- Don't use cedar or pine chips as litter or bedding because they can be toxic.
- Don't put the cage in direct sunlight, in the draft of an air-conditioning vent or room air-conditioner, or in any area where there is dampness such as in most cellars.
- Don't place the cage next to a television or stereo. Ferrets need to retreat to a quiet area when necessary.

A cage is like a den for ferrets. Because their ancestors were den animals, it is necessary to provide a private, den-like place for them to sleep. You may notice that your ferret sleeps 15 to 20 hours a day. As a matter of fact, ferrets sleep so soundly and relaxed that at times you might think that your pet has died. (Simply put your fingers against his chest and feel for a heartbeat.) You also will notice that your ferret adjusts his sleep schedule to suit your schedule. Your little companion will be eagerly waiting

Ferret Activity Cycle

Ferrets are diurnal, which means they are mostly active during the day. They sleep an average of 19 hours per day. However, despite the amount of time they like to sleep, it's not advisable to leave your pet in his cage for extended periods of time. If you do not allow him exercise and give him companionship on a daily basis, he will become stressed, unhappy, bored, and possibly difficult to handle.

Cage Maintenance Schedule

It's really not difficult to keep up with the rambunctious antics of a ferret, but here are a few tips to keep housekeeping matters under control:

- Change dry food and water daily.
- Change bedding every two to three days to help to keep odours under control.
- Scoop soiled litter from the litter box daily; clean and disinfect the litter box at least once a week.
- Clean up accidents on carpets and furniture using a solution made for pet stains. Always test any cleanser first to make sure that it doesn't affect the fabric's colour.

for you in the morning and at night when you arrive home.

Do not leave your ferret in his cage for extended periods of time; ferrets are not cage animals like hamsters, gerbils, mice, and rats. If you do not allow him exercise and give him love and companionship on a daily basis,

he will gain weight, develop stiff joints and muscles, become very stressed, unhappy, and bored, and may become difficult to handle.

Furnishings

Having the right cage is just the beginning. You also have to furnish it properly, as well as provide other items important to your ferret's health, comfort, and happiness. The following items are essential to proper care.

Food Dish

Most ferrets like to dump food or dig their food out of their food dish. Knowing this saves you a lot of hassle in picking the right food container for your pet. Dishes come in just about every size, shape, colour, and texture. A ceramic or weighted

Daily cage cleaning is vital to keeping your pets' home healthy, comfortable, and odour-free.

dish usually cannot be tipped over, but this type of dish can be moved around the cage. A better choice is a lock-on plastic crock-style food bowl. It's easy for you to remove and clean but still secure enough so that your ferret can't detach it from the cage. Avoid dishes made from flimsy plastic and those made from unglazed pottery. Stainless steel, thick plastic, and heavily glazed ceramic crock dishes work best.

Water Bottle

The best water bottles for ferrets are the size and type made for small animals (either 16 or 32 ounces). It's usually best to give a single ferret at least two bottles and to provide one more for each additional ferret living in the enclosure. The reason for doing this is that your pet will still have water if one of the bottles suddenly starts to leak or if it's too difficult for him to get water out of a sipper tube that has been blocked or has tremendous suction.

Attach a water bottle to the outside of the cage with the spout facing in. The sipper tube should be placed at a comfortable drinking level, about 6 to 8 inches (15.2 to 20.3 cm) from the floor of the cage. Clean the water bottle and the stainless steel sipper tube daily with hot, soapy water. Be sure to rinse it clean because any remaining soap can cause

upset tummy issues. Replace bottles as needed.

Litter Tray and Scoop

Ferrets tend to back into corners, raise their tails, and then do their business. It's best to use a tray with high sides (more than 4 inches [10.2 cm]). They do not need a tray with a low side because even kits and older ferrets can hop into one this height. High sides also help to contain litter and waste. Many people use plastic shoe boxes or plastic storage containers as litter trays in ferret cages.

To secure the litter box, drill some holes in the side of the box and secure it to the corner of the cage with wire or twist ties. This will keep your ferret from making a mess by flipping the box over or rearranging the cage. A metal or plastic scoop works well for

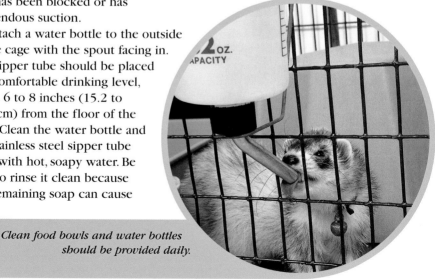

Clean food bowls and water bottles should be provided daily.

Homemade Toys

Keep in mind that some of the best pet toys don't come from a shop. No matter what you decide to give your ferret to play with, he will almost undoubtedly choose any object he finds interesting around the house.

Ferrets love playing with paper bags, cardboard boxes, empty containers, old socks with bells rolled up in them, drink bottles or PVC tubes taped together, or ping pong balls. Inspect all toys frequently, and discard any damaged ones.

cleaning out the soiled litter.

Litter

Pelleted products made from paper or plant fibres are excellent choices for ferret litter. These products are usually available at pet shops, feed shops, and at online pet sites.

Do not use scoopable litter. This type can irritate your ferret's eyes and may cause respiratory problems. Clay litter is dusty, offers little odour control, and may leave your ferret's coat feeling dry or tacky. Corncob litter is not very

absorbent, offers little odour control, and easily grows mould. Cedar and pine shavings may cause respiratory problems and make a real mess of the cage.

Bedding

Ferrets must have a nest-like environment for sleeping. If you do not provide one, your ferret may choose his own by burrowing inside places such as your sofa or a dresser drawer, or he will just sleep in a clean litter box under his ferret blanket.

Good choices for bedding include polar fleece baby blankets, cotton t-shirts, and sweatshirts. You also can purchase sleep sacks, hammocks, sleep cubes, and snooze tubes made especially for ferrets. Wash all bedding on a regular basis because much of the odour associated with a ferret is actually from the bedding and not from the ferret.

Toys

Ferrets love having their own toys, and they are necessary to their happiness and mental health. Be careful when choosing them, however. They should not have small pieces that can be bitten off and swallowed. Infant toys such as terry-covered soft rattles are good choices. Cat toys are also appropriate, although you need to be sure that they don't have any small, removable parts or contain foam stuffing that might cause digestive tract blockages.

Most ferrets are harder on toys than an animal such as a cat would be, so

Ferrets must have a nest-like environment for sleeping.

choose accordingly. Plastic balls, with or without bells, work well if they are not easily broken or swallowed (the little webbed ones break too easily). Hard rubber toys are fine, but be sure that they can't get stuck in your ferret's mouth, and always monitor their use and discard them when they start to crack. Avoid superballs because ferrets love to chew them to bits and eat the pieces. Squeaky toys for cats and dogs are acceptable if they're tough enough to stand up to chewing and can be easily squeaked. (Catnip won't hurt ferrets and won't affect them as it does cats.) Avoid soft rubber and vinyl toys; your ferret will chew these up quickly and might ingest the pieces.

Ferrets aren't really fussy. Most are just as happy playing in a paper bag, and they would even find the leg from an old pair of jeans fun to crawl through or nap in. Other household items that make good ferret toys include bathrobe belts, tennis balls, golf balls, ping-pong balls, film canisters (rinsed to wash out any chemicals), and old socks with bells rolled up in them.

Plastic shopping bags are popular, but supervise playtime to be sure that your pet doesn't suffocate or eat the plastic. Cardboard boxes are also fun, especially several nested together with ferret-sized holes cut out in various places. Plastic bottles can be turned into clear play tubes by cutting off their tops and taping them together. Carpet-roll tubes and tunnels made of plastic pipe, dryer hose, or black drainage tubing are popular too. Avoid tubes from toilet paper or paper towels, though; they're small enough that ferrets can get their heads stuck in them and choke or suffocate. An excellent, inexpensive toy is a piece of plastic dryer hose about 4 inches

(10 cm) in diameter. Wrap any loose wire ends. Be sure that your real dryer hose is out of reach (or get a metal one), because you're showing your pets that dryer hoses are great fun to crawl through. Clear dryer hose is even more fun, though less sturdy.

Dig boxes are great entertainment for ferrets because they love to burrow and dig. They can be made from just about anything. You can use large litter trays, large plastic tubs, plastic beverage and ice tubs, or a small kiddie pool. There are also many safe digging materials you can use. Switch these out every once in a while to keep your ferret stimulated:

• bio-degradable starch peanuts
• dirt
• sand
• plastic Easter eggs
• a mix of plastic ferret balls, rattle balls, wagon wheel toys, etc.
• scraps of fabric

No matter what you decide to give your ferret to play with, he will almost undoubtedly choose some household items you never expected as well. Keep anything that will be damaged by a little chewing, or that might hurt your pet, well out of reach. Unfortunately, activities like digging up houseplants or chewing on your best shoes can be enormous fun for a ferret, but there are things you can do to protect your possessions, which will be discussed later.

On a final note, ferrets like variety, and they get bored easily. Alternate

any toys you give your pet so that he always has something "new" to play with. If he hasn't seen a toy in several days, he'll react as if he's never seen it before. This helps to keep him stimulated and entertained.

Lead and Harness

If you plan to travel with your ferret or just take him outside with you, you will need to get him a harness and lead. The best type of harness is an H-shaped harness designed specifically for ferrets. You can find them at your local pet shop.

Proper fit is very important. Ferrets are the Houdini of companion pets and are great at escaping from ill-fitting harnesses. As long as you can fit

Toys will keep your ferret entertained, as well as giving him healthy exercise options.

Free Roaming vs. Caged Ferrets

Ferrets should be caged when not supervised for their own safety. Letting your ferret roam freely around the house requires constant and diligent ferret-proofing. Free-roaming ferrets are more difficult to toilet train; almost every corner in the house may need to have a litter box. A better solution is to have a ferret-safe room where your pet's cage is located. The ferret can come and go from the cage as he pleases and can safely play and exercise when he wants to. Some ferret owners opt for a ferret playpen instead of a cage, which allows their pet safe and sufficient exercise space 24/7. Free-roaming ferrets are not recommended for first-time owners who need more experience understanding ferret behaviours and ferret-proofing issues.

your little finger between the body and the harness, it is not too tight. Your furry friend will get used to wearing the harness fairly quickly. (See Chapter 6 for harness and lead training tips.)

Pet Carrier

Purchase a pet carrier for trips out of the house when you aren't using the harness and lead. A small- or medium-sized cat carrier is appropriate for one or two ferrets on a short trip. The medium-sized carrier is big enough to set up with a secured litter box (plastic shoe boxes work great), a hammock, bedding, lock-on food dish, and small (8 oz) water bottle.

To prevent accidents, it's always best to put your ferret in a carrier when you travel by car. Secure the carrier to the seat with a seat belt.

Ferret-Proofing Your Home

As every ferret owner knows, our little friends love to get into mischief. Whether your ferrets live in a cage when you're not around or roam free all the time, or whether they live in a single room or have the run of the house, the first line of defence for both your ferrets and for your possessions is a ferret-proofed home.

Openings

Never underestimate the ability of a ferret to get into trouble in a place that you thought was safe for him. Ferrets are able to "weasel" through the smallest of openings, and move extremely heavy objects out of their way if they think that there is something interesting just beyond their reach.

Ferrets love to "ferret" and so will worm their way into any little hole (as small as 2 x 2 inches [5.1 x 5.1 cm], or smaller for kits and some adults), which can be dangerous if the hole in question is under or behind a refrigerator or other appliance (with exposed wires, fans, and insulation), or if it leads into a wall or to the outdoors.

Crawl around on your stomach to look for holes near the floor and under cabinets, especially in the kitchen and laundry areas. Even holes inside cabinets should be blocked just in case. Also, watch out for heaters or furnace ducts.

Block openings with wood or wire mesh; be sure to leave ventilation around appliances, though. For blocking doorways, try a smooth piece of plywood or Plexiglas slid into brackets attached to the sides of the doorway.

Cabinets and Drawers

Holes aren't the only problem. Ferrets can open cabinets and drawers, which can be dangerous or just annoying, based on what's inside of them. Depending on how your cabinets and drawers are constructed—and how determined your ferrets are—you might be able to keep them closed using strong tape, rubber bands tied around a pair of handles, or a nail or wooden dowel through the handles. On a cabinet, you can use a strip of strong Velcro-type tape on the door and frame to keep it shut. Some types of child-proof lock also work very well, although others are too weak or will still open wide enough to let a ferret through.

Before you let your ferret out of his cage, be sure the area he is exploring has been pet-proofed.

Furniture

Recliners and sofa beds can be very dangerous; many ferrets have become crushed in the levers, springs, and frames inside or underneath them. Furniture is difficult to ferret-proof, except by putting it in an off-limits room.

Regular sofas and beds can be hazardous as well if a ferret digs or crawls his way into the springs or stuffing. If your pet scratches at the underside of your sofa to get through the fabric and into the bottom, try taking off the sofa's legs (if it has them). Heavy cloth or plywood stapled or nailed to the bottom can work, too, although ferrets often rip cloth loose. Sometimes they try to get into the bottom or arms of the sofa by burrowing between the cushions to the back or sides. This is much harder to prevent, but you can try blocking the area with cloth or wood that is stapled, nailed, taped, or sewn to the sofa frame under the cushioned seating. Many owners find it simpler to give up and get a futon or a sofa that doesn't have an inside in the first place.

On beds, many ferrets like to rip the cloth off the bottom of a box spring and climb into it, where they can easily get crushed or caught. To prevent this, try putting a fitted sheet on the bottom of your bed, anchored in place with small nails, or attach wire mesh or a thin piece of wood to the underside of the box spring. You may need to drill air holes in the wood so that the box spring can still compress.

Digging and Scratching

Digging is a favourite ferret pastime. Many like to dig at the carpet, especially near closed doors, and it's very difficult to teach them not to do it. You're better off protecting your carpet by putting down a piece of plastic carpet protector from an office supply shop. Chances are your ferret will get bored with digging when he sees he's

FAMILY-FRIENDLY TIP

Ferret Care Responsibility

Age and maturity are important factors when deciding how much responsibility a child can assume in caring for any pet. Parents of younger children must be aware that the animal's welfare will ultimately be their responsibility. Although children and ferrets can be wonderful playmates, parents should be willing to carefully monitor the pet's daily care. With adult supervision, children eight years of age and older can become a ferret owner, but just like with dogs or cats, a ferret should be considered a family pet rather than a child's pet. Never leave small children unsupervised with any animal, no matter how trusted the pet may be.

not getting anywhere, although it may take a while for that to happen. A carpet scrap or sample from a carpet shop might work, too, although your ferret will be able to shred it, so he may not give up as quickly.

For out-of-the-way places, wire mesh can be nailed to the floor through carpet, but avoid any sharp corners or points. Plants can be protected from digging (but not chewing) by putting large rocks or metal mesh over the tops of their pots.

Poison and Choking Hazards

You need to be vigilant about smaller items as well. Unfortunately, because ferrets will put anything into their mouths that seems interesting, accidents like choking, poisoning, and intestinal blockages may occur.

Apart from obvious dangers, such as bottles of toxic household cleaners (which ferrets do sometimes like to drink), be particularly careful with sponges, erasers, shoe insoles, foam earplugs, foam rubber (even inside a cushion or mattress), Styrofoam, insulation, rubber door stoppers, and anything else spongy or springy. Ferrets love to chew on these kinds of things. Also, watch your ferret's toys to make sure that they're not beginning to crack or break apart.

For some reason, many ferrets like to eat soap, so keep it away from your pet. (A little lick won't hurt your

ferret, but it may give him a bout of diarrhoea; large amounts can be a bigger problem.) Keep human foods out of reach because even the ones that aren't dangerous to ferrets, like fruits and vegetables, aren't good for them in large quantities.

Other Hazards

Next, look around the area in which your ferret will be playing. Put fragile items out of the way. Keep in mind that many ferrets are good climbers and jumpers, and they excel at finding complicated routes to places you never thought possible or within their reach. They can climb into a rubbish bin, onto the third shelf of a set of bookcases, or into the opening on the back of a stereo speaker. They also can unzip backpacks and purses, open boxes and containers, and climb up the sides

Ferrets need at least two hours outside their cage a day, so be vigilant about keeping your pets safe by supervising them at all times.

As a responsible owner, it's up to you to make sure your ferret has everything he needs to feel safe and comfortable in his new home.

of furniture from underneath or behind to get onto a desk, table, or kitchen worktop.

Be careful about full baths and sinks in which your ferret may possibly drown, and consider keeping your toilet lid closed for the same reason. Buckets of water, paint, etc. also can be drowning hazards, or they may simply create a mess if tipped over. Toilet paper and paper towel rolls are a problem because ferrets can get their heads stuck in them and choke or suffocate. If you let your ferret play with plastic bags, cut off the handles and cut a slit in the bottom to prevent him from suffocating.

Some ferrets have special hazard-proofing needs. For example, some like to eat paper or cloth, which can easily cause life-threatening intestinal blockages. Others may like to chew

on electrical cables, while some prefer plants. Be aware that quite a few common houseplants are poisonous to ferrets and other pets. Liberal application of a bitter apple paste to these items can help to persuade your pet to stop gnawing on them.

Keep in mind that even *you* can be dangerous to your ferret. Always double-check your dishwasher, refrigerator, washing machine, and dryer (even top-loading models) before closing them or turning them on, and watch where you sit and walk—that chair, throw rug, or pile of laundry might be concealing a napping ferret.

Finally, once your home is done, it's important to keep it safe. Ferret-proofing is not something that is done once and then forgotten about. It is a constant chore to stay one step ahead of these furry bandits.

Home Safety Checklist

- Look at your home from a ferret's point-of-view. Crawl around on your stomach to look for holes near the floor and under cabinets, especially in the kitchen and laundry area.
- Recliners and sofa beds are very dangerous; many ferrets have become crushed in the levers and springs underneath.
- Be careful about full baths, where your ferret might possibly drown, and consider keeping your toilet lid closed for the same reason.
- Always double-check your dishwasher, refrigerator, and washing machine and dryer (even top-loading models) before closing them or turning them on, and watch where you sit and walk—that chair, throw rug, or pile of laundry might be hiding a napping ferret.
- Make sure that all hazardous household items are securely stored away.
- Remove poisonous houseplants, or keep them out of reach.
- Keep toenails trimmed. Long or split nails can get hooked on many materials, causing a ferret to become trapped or to do harm to himself to escape. Your veterinarian can show you how to trim them properly.
- Keep your ferret's environment and bedding clean and fresh. Avoid using strong or harsh-smelling cleaners, and be sure to rinse everything thoroughly.
- Find a reliable veterinarian who treats ferrets in your area. Post her telephone number in a conspicuous place for emergencies. Also, find out the doctor's procedure for after-hours emergencies.
- Always take your ferret to the veterinarian if he is not behaving normally. Ferrets are so small that they can become dehydrated and overcome by illness rapidly. When in doubt, check it out!

Chapter 3

Good Eating

Good nutrition is a necessary requirement for maintaining a healthy ferret. Providing your pet with the proper diet and nutrition, then, is of the utmost importance—not to mention that ferrets love to eat!

Natural Diet

Ferrets are obligate carnivores. In their natural environment, they eat whole prey. This includes all parts of the killed animal. They do not eat grains, fruits, and vegetables because they cannot digest the fibre present in these foods. However, they may get a tiny amount of them from what their prey has just eaten.

Food passes through the ferret rather quickly, so they eat small amounts several times throughout the day and will stash extra food away to be eaten later. Ferrets get their energy from fat (not carbohydrates) and from meat protein (not vegetable protein) and so require a diet that is highly concentrated with fat, has highly digestible meat, and includes minimal carbohydrates.

Because ferrets in their natural setting are predators of small animals, the most balanced and natural diet to feed them is a whole prey diet. Appropriately sized prey animals include mice, rats, quail, and chicks. Today, these items can be purchased easily frozen or live. The next best choice to feeding a whole prey diet is to feed a naturally prepared ferret food, such as a balanced, raw carnivore diet. Many pet food companies are realising that heat-processed foods may not be the answer for a natural diet and have responded by developing raw, balanced, organic pet foods. These diets are available freeze-dried and frozen.

Never feed wild-caught prey or any dead wild prey animals. This puts your ferret at risk of contracting dangerous

Ferret Feeding Guidelines

Tips for good ferret nutrition include the following:

- Offer foods that have high animal protein and fat content (35–40 percent protein and at least 20 percent fat).
- Do not feed vegetables or fruits.
- Make food available all the time.
- Supply plenty of fresh water daily.
- Provide supplements only if needed.
- Keep treats to a minimum, and make sure that they're healthy.

bacteria and parasites. If you want your pet to go on a more natural diet, consult your veterinarian first.

Basic Nutrition

Much has been learned in recent years about what ferrets need for a long and healthy life. Many commercial pet food manufacturers are now finally addressing the ferret's unique feeding requirements. Until recently, the common recommendation from vets and breeders was to feed good-quality dry cat or kitten food, but that recommendation is now considered out of date. As we've seen from their diet in the wild, ferrets, like cats, are carnivores. Food passes through their digestive system very quickly, so they lack the ability to derive much nutrition from plant matter. For this reason, a domestic ferret diet must be high in animal protein, relatively high in fat, and low in fibre. All foods, including foods intended solely for ferrets, are not created equally, so be careful what you feed your pet.

The domestic ferret diet staple mainly consists of dry processed foods. This is the easiest and most convenient type of diet you can offer. When choosing a dry food, read the label closely to make sure that the ingredients are the best you can get. Much has been done to improve the quality of these dry diets so that they are appropriate for the ferret's unique dietary needs;

however, many still contain large quantities of carbohydrates and sugars that can be detrimental to the long-term health of your pet. Be sure that the main ingredients are high-quality meat-based products.

Required Nutrients

When choosing commercial foods, look at the nutrient analysis on the packaging; it will list the minimum levels of protein and fat in the diet. You also need to examine the ingredient list carefully. Protein can come from a variety of sources, including plant matter, so make sure that the bulk of the protein is derived from meat and poultry products. Chicken or poultry meal and egg are high-quality protein sources and are good choices.

37

Your ferret will need a nutritionally balanced diet to stay healthy.

Many pet foods, especially the inexpensive types, use corn as a major source of protein, but this will be largely indigestible to your ferret. Again, always choose foods that are high in fat and low in carbohydrates.

The list of ingredients on most packaging is based on content percentages in the food, from greatest to least. Appropriate ferret foods should have 35 to 40 percent protein and no less than 20 percent fat. Your best bet is to look for diets with meat or egg products making up at least four of the first six listed ingredients. Also, chicken fat is considered a better-balanced fat source than other animal sources.

Also, just because a bag of food has a picture of a ferret on it does not mean that it offers your pet a good diet. Many products on the market today should never be fed to ferrets. Do not feed any diet that contains pieces of dried fruit, dried vegetables, fruit

Diet Differences

Kibble Diets:
- These should be available at all times. Feed 1/4 to 1/2 cup daily.
- Ferrets will eat several times throughout the day (usually every three to four hours).

Fresh or Prey Diets:
- These should be fed twice daily.
- Amount fed should be no more than what a ferret will consume at each feeding.
- Remove uneaten food promptly.

Healthy Diet Benefits

If your ferret is eating a well-balanced and nutritious diet:
- His fur will be soft and shiny.
- His eyes will be bright and clear.
- His skin will be soft.
- He will have a high activity level.
- He will have well-formed droppings that won't smell too bad.
- He will be very happy.

juices, sugar, cornmeal, or corn-gluten meal. If you do feed diets with these ingredients, expect your pet to have a shortened life either by disease or from a blockage caused by these unhealthy foods.

As the science of ferret nutrition improves, there is little doubt that premium diets are the best kibble diets to feed. Still, if you are unable to find a good-quality ferret food (consider ordering online if nothing else), you may have to settle for cat food. If so, make sure that it is the best you can offer (preferably made with chicken and little to no fish). Use a kitten food high in protein and fat. Be careful introducing high protein (50 percent) diets, either cat or ferret, to older ferrets. Because they are not used to the high protein, you may be doing more harm than good. If your ferret has been raised on a high-protein diet, however, he should be fine continuing on it throughout his lifetime.

Feeding Schedule

Ferrets have a quick metabolism along with a short digestive system, so they need to eat frequently (usually every three to four hours). It is best to have food available at all times. Your ferret will eat about 1/4 to 1/2 cup of a kibble diet daily. If you have more than one ferret, be sure to have a big enough food dish (or several) and enough food so that everyone gets their fill.

Most ferrets will eat only enough to meet their needs and will not become obese if allowed constant access to good-quality food. If you are having a problem with your ferret gaining too much weight, check with a vet to rule out medical problems and for advice on meeting his nutritional needs while maintaining a good weight.

Changing Dietary Needs

Regardless of why you may be changing your ferret's food, always make any diet changes slowly, mixing in the new food with the old and gradually reducing the amount of the old diet. It is often a good idea to use a mixture of food types beginning when your ferret is young because some can be stubborn about trying new foods, which may create problems later if his current food becomes unavailable. Also, at some point, if your ferret

The domestic ferret diet mainly consists of dry processed foods.

becomes ill or simply begins ageing, it will be helpful to transition to different feeding regimens more easily.

Ferrets usually do not need soft food unless they are ill or very young. With that said, kits who are weaned properly and who are mature enough to be away from their mother should be starting to eat meat by three-and-a-half weeks of age and crunching on their mom's kibble by five weeks of age. Tinned diets are not recommended as a regular diet, but it's good to get your ferret used to eating them. It is much easier to mix medicine in a soft food or use it for syringe feeding when necessary.

Up to one year of age, ferrets should be fed a high-protein and high-fat diet. From one to four years of age, you can drop the fat percentage only if your ferret is getting a bit pudgy. Most do not become overweight from their regular diet. Ferrets over four years of age still can be fed their regular diet unless they start having kidney problems. Dropping the protein level will help in this case.

Water

A ferret should have fresh water available at all times—both inside and outside of the cage. Be sure to change the water daily. Inside the enclosure, a water bottle made for small animals

The Expert Knows

Got Water?

Make fresh water available at all times. Water helps to deliver vital nutrients to the cells in your ferret's body, and it removes waste. It also helps to keep your pet hydrated and healthy.

Offer fresh water daily in a clean water bottle with a sipper tube. Water bowls are not the best choice in the cage because they are too easily contaminated with bedding or other cage debris as your pet scampers around his home. To help to maintain your pet's good health, wash and rinse the water bottle daily to ensure that it remains free of germs and mould, and inspect it regularly to make sure that your pet isn't chewing on the stopper and causing it to leak. Hang extra bottles on cages with multiple ferrets.

attached to the side of the cage often works best. A bowl is okay for use outside the cage, but make sure that it is heavy enough not to flip over. Most ferrets will make a fun but messy game of playing in their water bowl.

Ferrets on a kibble diet have to have a constant supply of water. The volume of water required is about three times the volume of kibble eaten. In warm weather, your ferret will drink much more than usual. Ferrets who can't drink won't eat.

Commercial Ferret Foods

Several commercial ferret diets are available now, and some are better than others. Good diets tend to be expensive but are worth the additional cost. Some foods are simply modified cat or mink diets, which may be no more appropriate than a high-quality cat food. Be careful to check the labels. Be warned that fish-based diets tend to make your pet and his litter tray smelly, and some ferrets may not like them.

The best kibble diet for your ferret should meet the following criteria:

- Protein should be meat based and between 35 and 40 percent.
- Fat content should be at least 20 percent.
- Fibre content should be 3 percent or less.
- Corn should not be listed in the first 3 ingredients.
- Meat should be listed instead of meat by-products.
- Fish shouldn't be listed in the first 6 ingredients.

Human Foods

With proper research and preparation, a fresh diet is an excellent way to make sure that your ferret is eating right. It will have few, if any, chemicals or preservatives, and plenty of good-quality ingredients tailored to his specific needs. But providing your ferret with a noncommercial diet is a commitment that takes time, education, and dedication, or you will shortchange his nutrition. If you are willing to put

in the extra effort, your ferret's good health will be your reward. Here are some basic guidelines:

- Try chopping up small pieces of chicken or turkey, and allow your ferret to taste them. You can use cooked or raw poultry; if using raw, you can include bones.
- Chicken or beef liver and hearts are great treats and are very nutritious for your ferret.
- Offer natural meat juices. Use a small bowl or drizzle them over kibble.

Don't expect a change overnight. Persistence and experimentation are the keys to converting your ferret to a more natural diet. Let's discuss the options.

The Raw Diet

Many people believe that ferrets should eat the way nature intended, and so they opt for a BARF (biologically

Regardless of why you may be changing your ferret's food, always make any transitions slowly to avoid digestive upset.

Supplements

Ferretone and Linatone are two popular vitamin supplements given to ferrets. They are also one of the most common treats offered because nearly every ferret loves them. They're very similar and can be used interchangeably, although their exact composition is a bit different. Both of these contain vitamin A, which can be very harmful or even fatal in excess, (although it probably takes a whole lot more than you'd ever give a ferret). Still, some people prefer to dilute them 50/50 with olive oil or vegetable oil (*not* mineral oil), which shouldn't hurt. Also, as with hairball remedies, too much Ferretone or Linatone can give your ferrets loose stools. No more than a few drops to one pump a day is recommended.

Similarly, many people give their ferrets a small amount of a cat hairball remedy such as Laxatone or Petromalt on a regular basis. These can help them pass Styrofoam, rubber bands, and other such items that ferrets seem to love to eat, as well as help to prevent hairballs from fur swallowed during grooming. Even better, most ferrets seem to think of this as a wonderful treat, too. As with all treats and supplements, give them only in moderation; you can estimate how much by taking the recommended cat dosage and adjusting it for a ferret's smaller weight. Your best bet is to always check with your vet before giving your pet any supplements or over-the-counter medications to see what she recommends.

Supplements are not thought to be necessary at all if you're using a good food.

appropriate raw food) diet. BARF diets have long been common practice in Europe and Australia.

Raw chicken and rabbit are the most common meat choices given to ferrets on a BARF diet. Common-sense precautions, like thawing frozen meat in the refrigerator instead of at room temperature, lessen the risk of bacterial infection. In addition, there is a greater chance of contracting parasites from wild-caught prey than from properly handled human-grade meat.

Raw food should be left raw.

Microwaving it—even as briefly as 30 seconds—damages live enzymes and hardens the bones. And speaking of bones, *cooked* poultry bones are dangerous. Raw bones don't splinter; they crunch into small pieces that help to clean your ferret's teeth. They are also a good source of calcium and phosphorus.

There are no magic cures for physical ailments, but many BARFers think that a raw diet is the next best thing. Allergies and other skin conditions, inflammatory bowel disease

(IBD), and other gastrointestinal conditions often disappear after transitioning to a raw diet. If you want your ferret to go raw, consult your ferret-knowledgeable veterinarian first. For more information on natural ferret diets, check out the Natural Ferret Yahoo Group at NaturalFerrets@ yahoogroups.com.

Cooked Diets

If you are not comfortable feeding a more natural diet, or you've tried feeding it and your ferret looked at you like you were crazy, maybe a cooked or partially cooked diet is right for you and your pet.

One of the first chicken gravy recipes for ferrets was developed by ferret expert, researcher, and fancier Bob Church. This recipe has been circulated on the Internet and modified hundreds of times. It is nutritious and digests easily. It is also a good source of nutrition for a ferret that is ill or a senior who may not be able to deal with solid food. Here is a modified version that I recommend:

Kerry's Chicken Gravy

(based on Bob Church's Chicken Recipe; courtesy of Kerry Fabrizio)

> 2 chickens (with giblets)
> 2 cups chicken livers
> double handful, about half-pound, of fat trimmings (I use chicken, but you can use beef or pork) or use a small block of lard.
> 4 eggs
> 2 cups water
> 2 to 3 tbsp. Ferretone
> 2 to 3 tbsp. light olive oil
> 2 tubes Nutri-Cal or Nutri-Stat
> 6 tbsp. honey
> *Optional: A whole rabbit can be added to the mix, just increase the water to 3 cups. You can also add chicken hearts and gizzards or necks and backs. If you are trying to entice a ferret to try the gravy, you*

A diet high in fat and protein and very low in fibre is ideal for ferrets.

can add ground kibble to the mix to add a familiar smell. After they have accepted the gravy as food, you no longer need to add the kibble.

You'll also need a good Chinese cleaver or knife (depending on your skill level), a big, heavy cutting board, and a hand or electric meat grinder.

Note: Cook the chicken "wet." This means it is mixed with water if ground first, or in water if cooked first. Bones cooked wet are not brittle like bones cooked dry, so this is much safer for your ferret, especially when feeding chunk-style so they can chew up the bones.

How much meat you chop up will depend on your ferrets (how much they eat and what consistency they prefer). To begin, cut the meat off the bones with scissors or a knife, grind it

with the grinder on the largest grind size, and then toss it in a big pot. Next, chop up most of the bones with a cleaver or knife, which does a great job of cutting them up. Grind drumsticks because they tend to splinter (they can easily be omitted if you feel more comfortable). Process the eggs in a blender or food processor until the shells become very tiny pieces, and then add the fat trimmings, extra gizzards, livers, and hearts. Process the mixture until everything is ground up.

Note: For ferrets that have never eaten the gravy, you may want to process the mixture more to make it mushier. Try it this way and see how your ferrets take to it. Initially, I started out cooking, cutting, and grinding the ingredients, and then putting them through the blender on puree. Over

Ferrets have a quick metabolism along with a short digestive system, so they need to eat frequently.

Unhealthy Foods

If you want your ferret to live a longer, healthier life, there are certain foods you should never give him.

Do not feed your ferret fruits or vegetables. These can lead to malnutrition, diarrhoea, and gastrointestinal blockages if he eats too much of them. Ferrets cannot digest vegetable matter. Even a small piece of fruit or vegetable can cause a bowel obstruction and endanger the life of your pet.

Also, do not feed your ferret dairy products, sweets, nuts, chocolate, licorice, soda, rawhide, or any sugary or salty snacks. Besides the usual tummy upset, some of these items can cause serious health problems and even death. Most are indigestible to a ferret. Dairy products can cause gastrointestinal upset. Sugar can interfere with the function of the pancreas, which can lead to insulinoma disease. (Don't even think that only one raisin or one piece of toasted oat cereal is okay for your ferret.) Because ferrets can become very ill from having too much salt, never feed seasoned table scraps. It goes without saying, but caffeine and alcohol are also off-limits.

the years, I got to the point that all I needed to do was cut it and cook it. You may get to the point that you don't need the grinder at all.

Once ground, put the mixture of meat and meat ingredients into a pot with the water and cook it to 170°F (77°C) (use a thermometer). Once it's done, take it off the heat, cool, and add all the additional ingredients. Stir it up, put it in containers after it cools, and freeze.

To serve, let one container thaw in the fridge (usually overnight), put some in a dish, heat lightly, maybe with some extra water or chicken stock to make it juicy, and let your ferrets try it. If they won't eat it, don't despair.

Try more mincing, chopping, or blending, add more juice, stick their paws or nose in it, and just keep trying until you arrive at a blend they enjoy.

Note: Getting your ferrets to the point that they are willing to eat the gravy chunky has great dental benefits! This may take time with older ferrets. Kits take to it very quickly and will prefer the chunks to the ground version.

If your ferret is used to an all-kibble diet, he may not like the chicken gravy at first. You can try to syringe feed him some or let him lick it from a spoon. It may take some time, but most ferrets eventually come around and will eat the gravy on their own – and may actually like it! Once he starts eating the gravy, it is then very easy to get him to eat chicken and turkey without the gravy. I imprint all my kits on meat this way, and they are meat eaters for life.

You can make eating gravy more of a game by serving it in an eggshell prior to serving the whole meal. Put a tablespoon full or so in half an eggshell. This way each ferret has his own serving and they will all get an equal share. If your ferret ends up eating the eggshell, don't worry. It contains good minerals and will not hurt him.

Chicken gravy isn't a replacement for your ferret's regular diet or

Healthy Treats

Treats, no matter how healthy, should always be given in moderation. You want to be sure that your pet will eat his regular diet so that his nutritional balance is not disrupted, which may weaken his immune system and thus make him more susceptible to illness.

Instead of snacks that may be high in sugar, there are other alternatives such as bite-sized pieces of meat or vitamin supplements that ferrets love to eat. Besides being tasty, treats provide an added benefit: They make great training aids, too. Some suggestions for healthy treats include:

- chicken, turkey, steak (cooked or raw)
- homemade jerky treats
- freeze-dried liver treats
- cooked eggs
- creamy peanut butter
- Ferretvite and Ferretone

Although ferrets enjoy treats, they should be given in limited quantities.

anything your vet may prescribe such as duck soup or any other foods, but lots of experienced owners do swear by it and do supplement their ferret's diet with some sort of gravy. If your ferret doesn't like something in the recipe, feel free to modify and adjust it to meet your individual's particular needs.

Treats

Ferrets love treats. Small amounts of goodies won't hurt, but be sure that you don't fill your ferret up on them because he'll need to eat his regular food to get the required amounts of protein and fat for a balanced and complete diet.

The best treats for your ferret are meat based. Cooked chicken, turkey, and steak are healthy choices. Never give your ferret any fruits (fresh or dried) or high carb sugary foods such as raisins, toasted oat cereal, or anything banana-raisin flavoured. Commercial treats like Ferretone and Ferretvite should be used in strict moderation. Use them sparingly. Provide no more than 1 inch (2.5 cm) of the paste or several drops of the liquid only once or twice a week—too much of either of these can cause problems.

Special Needs

Obesity

Obesity is not common in ferrets who are fed a high-quality diet. Some ferrets tend to get heavier with age, and most put on extra weight in the winter. This winter weight gain is normal.

A healthy adult male should weigh from 2 to 5 pounds (0.9 to 2.3 kg), and a female will weigh about half that. Ferrets, especially males, tend to gain weight in the winter and then lose it again in the spring.

Like humans, ferrets can have different body types. Some just have a stockier build than others, which can make one appear heavier than another longer and leaner ferret.

When you run your hand down your ferret's side, you should feel his muscles ripple a bit and be able to feel his ribs, but they shouldn't stick out and he shouldn't feel too bony. If your ferret feels soft and "pudgy" or looks pear shaped, he might be overweight or just have poor muscle tone due to insufficient exercise. Try letting him exercise more often and for longer periods of time, and cut back a bit on his food.

Senior Diets

Ferrets over four years of age who are fed an all-kibble diet can be switched to a food with a lower protein level. (Kibble diets high in protein can be detrimental to proper kidney function in seniors.) These diets also contain adequate levels of taurine, an amino acid that plays an important part in maintaining vision and a healthy heart. There are now ferret diets on the market that are manufactured to meet a senior ferret's nutritional needs.

Feeding the Sick or Elderly Ferret

Feeding your ferret when he becomes sick or stops eating his regular diet can be a challenge, even for the most experienced owner. A recipe recommended by many vets and breeders for ill or elderly individuals, and one that you should have on hand, is for

Ferrets

The amount you feed will vary depending on age, activity level, and weight.

"Duck Soup." This homemade recipe was named after Lucky Duck, the ferret for whom it was originally created when he was sick and needed something nutritional to eat.

Duck Soup

- 1 can canine/feline prescription diet
- 3 to 4 oz. 100 percent pure pumpkin, mashed
- 1 tbsp. of an all-natural ferret supplement
- 2 tsp. of a pro-biotic digestive tract supplement for ferrets
- 2/3 cup ground-up regular diet dry kibble softened with water additional water as needed

Mix all of the ingredients together, adding warm water to create an appropriate consistency for feeding: soupy or thick enough for a syringe, whatever consistency your ferret likes.

If your ferret is strong enough and finds the food appealing, offer it in a shallow bowl or let him lick it from a spoon. Most ferrets love the extra attention during spoon feedings.

If your ferret will not freely eat on his own, you will probably need to syringe feed him. You can purchase a feeding syringe from your vet or local pet shop. Suck some of the softened food into the syringe, then squeeze a small amount into the corner of your ferret's mouth. Be sure to feed him slowly and in small amounts; you don't want your pet to

FAMILY–FRIENDLY TIP

Supervise Feeding

A child can help a parent fill up the ferret's food dish and change the water bottle daily. Although kids should not be the only ones responsible for feeding a ferret, it's a good idea to have them take an active daily role in this part of the family pet's care. Children aged ten and older usually can assume almost full responsibility, although parents should still oversee care to make sure that the pet is properly fed.

choke. Don't give up—you may end up with more food on you and your ferret than in him. Just make sure that he eats several good cc's (cubic centimetres) of food five to six times a day until he is once again eating on his own.

For more information about healthy diets for ferrets visit the British Ferret Club's website at www.britishferretclub.co.uk and the National Ferret Welfare Society at www.nfws.net.

Good Eating

Chapter 4

Looking Good

Grooming and good hygiene are an important part of your responsibilities as a pet owner. Regular grooming not only keeps your ferret looking good, but it also can help to keep him feeling good. A regular hands-on routine also gives you an opportunity to look for subtle changes in his appearance or body that may signal a health problem, as well as provide social time that will strengthen the bond you share.

I f you're looking for a pet who requires little in the way of grooming, ferrets are a good choice. Their grooming needs are actually quite simple. They're pretty much "wash-and-wear" animals who need very little to maintain a tidy appearance.

Brushing

While always a good idea, brushing is not as necessary with ferrets as it is with many other pets. Nevertheless, regular brushing is a great way to keep your pet's coat in top condition. It will help to remove dead hairs and will keep the coat glossy and shiny by distributing natural oils from the skin.

Many ferrets are not keen on staying still long enough for grooming, so get into the habit of doing frequent quick brushing sessions rather than trying to get your squirmy pal to sit calmly for a prolonged grooming routine. Use a soft short-bristled or pin-style brush meant for cats or kittens, or try one of the newer rubber grooming tools, which are great at picking up loose hair from the coat.

Brushing is also especially useful during shedding season to minimise the amount of loose hair your ferret could ingest, thus preventing hairballs that can cause problems ranging from upset tummies to intestinal blockages. Because ferrets do not vomit up hairballs like cats do, severe intestinal blockages could be potentially fatal. If your ferret exhibits poor or intermittent appetite, coughing, vomiting, or weight loss, take him to your veterinarian right away. She will determine if your pet does indeed have a hairball and whether surgery is necessary to remove it. Aside from regular grooming, you can use a hairball preventive. Give your ferret about half a teaspoon of

Regular grooming not only keeps your ferret looking good, but it improves his overall hygiene and health.

Grooming Supplies

These are the grooming supplies you will need for your ferret:

- soft short-bristled or pin-style brush
- ferret or kitten shampoo
- human or cat nail clippers
- styptic powder
- cotton swabs
- ferret or kitten ear cleaner
- petroleum jelly or pad protectant
- Ferretone or Linatone
- hairball preventive
- soft finger brush, gauze, or a child's toothbrush
- toothpaste formulated for ferrets, cats, or kittens

the medication once or twice a week during the shedding period. You do not need to administer this year round.

Bathing

A lot of controversy exists about when and how often to bathe ferrets. Although people who are sensitive to their naturally musky scent may be tempted or advised to bathe their animals more often, frequent bathing is not recommended. Most experts agree that ferrets should not be bathed more than once a month, and most can go four to six months between baths, unless of course they get into a mess and need to be tidied up.

Your ferret's scent is partially due to the oils from his skin, so a bath may temporarily reduce odour. However, because bathing strips the skin and fur of these oils, it will actually stimulate the musk glands to compensate for the loss by increasing production of more oils to moisturise and protect skin that has become dry. As a result, the musky scent actually may become even stronger for a couple of days after the bath. Keeping the cage and litter clean will better keep your furry friend smelling fresh.

How to Bathe Your Ferret

The first few encounters with bath time will set the tone for future baths. Some ferrets take quite naturally to water, while others are very reluctant to get into a bath. If your ferret seems afraid of the water, take it slow and be very patient. Try to keep the experience as stress-free as possible. If you are stressed, your ferret will pick up on this, so keep your tone upbeat, offer some favourite treats, and perhaps provide a few fun waterproof toys. Making bath time more like a special playtime may help things go more smoothly. Be aware that if your pet is new at this and has not relieved himself prior to bathing, he may do his "business" in the bath water in the excitement of the moment.

When you need to bathe your ferret, have everything ready before

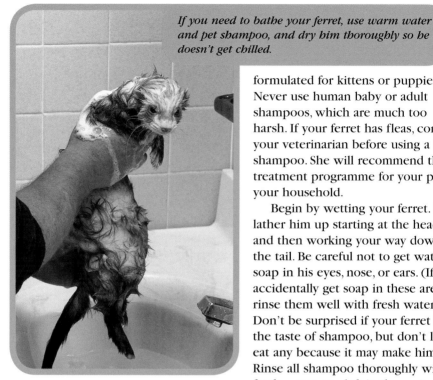

If you need to bathe your ferret, use warm water and pet shampoo, and dry him thoroughly so he doesn't get chilled.

formulated for kittens or puppies. Never use human baby or adult shampoos, which are much too harsh. If your ferret has fleas, consult your veterinarian before using a flea shampoo. She will recommend the best treatment programme for your pet and your household.

Begin by wetting your ferret. Next, lather him up starting at the head and then working your way down to the tail. Be careful not to get water or soap in his eyes, nose, or ears. (If you accidentally get soap in these areas, rinse them well with fresh water.) Don't be surprised if your ferret likes the taste of shampoo, but don't let him eat any because it may make him sick. Rinse all shampoo thoroughly with fresh water; any left in the coat could be drying or irritating. Refill the tub again if necessary to make sure that the rinse is as complete as possible.

you start: shampoo, towels, etc. You can bathe him in a bath or kitchen sink; the depth and height of a kitchen sink usually offers the most convenience. Fill the bath or sink with just enough water that your ferret is mostly covered but is still able to stand on the bottom. Use water that feels slightly warm to the touch but is not too hot. Be careful to support your pet properly during the bath because this will help him feel secure and safe.

Use a gentle shampoo. Your best bet is to buy one made specifically for ferrets; there are several brands and scents available. If you can't find a ferret-specific shampoo, use one

Does My Ferret Need a Bath?

While good hygiene is important, it is equally important not to bathe your ferret too frequently. Bathing too often will result in dry, flaky skin and a dry, coarse coat. Unless your ferret gets into something nasty and gets very dirty, do not bathe him more than once a month at the most.

Towel drying is usually sufficient to remove excess water. Ferrets naturally tend to dry off quickly, but do not allow your pet to become chilled while he's still damp. Also, unless the cage has just been cleaned, don't put him in there while he's still damp—a romp through a dirty cage and/or litter box will undo the work of the bath. Give your ferret a fresh, dry towel and watch him play with it for awhile—ferrets get pretty frisky after a bath. Some are okay being dried with a blow dryer, but if you choose to try this, keep the dryer on a low setting and at least 1 foot (0.3 m) away from the body.

If you find your ferret's slight odour unpleasant even after the bath, you might consider purchasing a portable air cleaner. It will remove odours and dander from the air. You can install a permanent air filter that fits into the heating/cooling system of your house. You also might want to consider removing the carpeting from your ferret area.

Nail Care

Proper nail care is an important part of your ferret's grooming programme. Nails need to be clipped on a regular basis (every two weeks), not only to prevent you from getting scratched but as protection for your ferret. Long nails can get caught in towels, bedding, carpeting, or on cage parts, and they also place undue stress on the joints of the paws.

The optimal time to clip nails is when your ferret is tired or has been sleeping, not when he is at his busiest. It's often best to have someone help you while you do the clipping. A helper can grasp your ferret by the scruff of the neck and keep him restrained, giving you easier access to the paws. For more stability, the lower body should be supported on your helper's lap or on a countertop.

To trim nails, use a pair of human or cat nail clippers. Before you begin, take your ferret's paw in your hand, gently grasp each nail, and look for the blood

Declawing—Not!

Declawing is a surgical procedure that involves the removal of the claw and the bone to which it is attached. Ferrets should never be declawed, but they do need to have their nails clipped regularly. Unlike cats, they do not retract their claws or use a scratching post to keep their nails trimmed.

Ferrets need their nails for various daily activities, such as grasping onto objects and moving them around, climbing and lowering themselves, grooming, eating, and even just to remove particles of food that sometimes get caught in the roof of their mouth. Therefore, do not consider declawing your pet under any circumstances.

vein area called the quick. It is easy to see in bright light. Most ferrets have light or translucent nails, and the quick is visible as the pink part inside the nail. Make your cut a bit in front of the quick; if you get too close, it may be painful for your ferret.

No matter how careful you are, at some point you will likely hit the quick accidentally and cause some bleeding. Don't panic; just make sure that you have something on hand to stop the bleeding, like a commercial styptic powder product. These sometimes sting but are highly effective. Take a pinch of powder, and press it onto the tip of the affected nail after wiping away the blood. Cornflour or flour also can be used in a similar manner. For minor bleeding, simply applying pressure to the tip of the nail may be sufficient.

Regardless of which method you use, make sure that the bleeding has stopped before placing your ferret back in his cage or leaving him unattended.

If you don't have a helper, you can try enlisting the aid of a fatty acid supplement (either Ferretone or Linatone) to make the job a bit easier. Scruff your ferret by the back of the neck and recline him in your lap, belly up. Place several drops of the supplement on his belly and put his nose in it. While your ferret is busy licking it up and happily distracted, you can release the scruff and cut his nails. Some ferrets eat faster than others, so you may need to apply more supplement to finish the job. If your pet has never had Ferretone or Linatone before, introduce him to the product gradually before attempting to cut his nails.

56

Long nails can cause your ferret injury and impair his ability to walk correctly, so trim them regularly.

Paws and Pads

Once your ferret's nails have been trimmed, examine his paws and pads. Aside from being vulnerable to injury, their condition may suffer from problems associated with illness or ageing. Older ferrets, for example, may have dry and thickened pads. Rubbing a tiny bit of petroleum jelly on them (or a product made for use on a pet's pads) will help to ease dryness and cracking.

Clip your ferret's nails frequently. If clipping becomes part of your regular routine, he will eventually get used to the procedure (and so will you), and you will just have to trim a little bit off the tip of the nail each time. For safety, don't forget to gently restrain your ferret during every nail trimming session.

If you have any doubts about how to do this procedure properly, ask a professional groomer, veterinarian, or experienced ferret owner to demonstrate clipping for you before you attempt it on your own.

Ear Care

Check your ferret's ears at least once a week. By inspecting them and keeping them clean and dry, you can prevent any problems from becoming chronic. Ferrets tend to have waxy ears. Normally, their earwax is light brown or reddish in colour. Regular cleaning will help you spot a change in the colour or in the amount or texture of earwax, which could indicate an infection or ear mites.

To clean the ears, get a mild ear cleaning solution made specifically for ferrets from your vet or pet shop; one safe for kittens should be okay as well. You can use a small amount of peroxide on occasion, but do not use alcohol because it can cause dryness and may sting on contact. Put a few drops in the ear, massage it for a bit, then clean the excess with a cotton swab. Be sure to only clean the external part of the ear. Never push a cotton swab into the ear canal; if your ferret is

FAMILY-FRIENDLY TIP

Grooming Instructions for Kids

As with any aspect of pet care, children can assist with grooming chores if an adult monitors them. Youngsters can help to groom a ferret on occasion by gently brushing him for a brief session. After demonstrating that they can handle the ferret carefully without harming him, they can be allowed to groom him regularly. Children also can look at the ferret's eyes or ears to see if they need cleaning and let an adult know if special attention is required. Other responsibilities can be added as children mature.

Dental Care

Healthy teeth are essential to proper nutrition and good hygiene, and ferrets have lots of them. Young kits have 30 baby teeth, which erupt between 20 and 28 days of age. Adults have 34 teeth, which erupt between 50 and 74 days of age.

There are four main types of teeth. The small upper and lower incisors located in the front are used to gather food. The canines, also called the fang or eye teeth, are used to puncture food. The premolars are used to shear or cut the food, and the molars are used to grind up the food.

Like human teeth, ferrets' teeth can build up plaque and tarter that, if left untreated, will eventually lead

particularly squirmy, be extra cautious to avoid pushing wax farther down into the ear.

Ear mites are quite common, and ear infections can occur on occasion as well. Take your ferret to the vet as soon as possible to rule out problems if he has excessive earwax or discharge; dark brown or black wax; bad-smelling ears; or if he is shaking his head, scratching at the ears, rubbing the side of his head on the cage or bedding, or tilting his head to the side often.

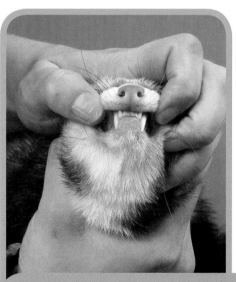

To prevent dental problems and ensure proper nutrition, have your pet's teeth cleaned on a regular basis.

If you begin grooming your ferret while he is young, he will grow accustomed to regular handling.

to tooth decay and gum disease. Feeding mostly dry food and avoiding sugary treats will help, but even with proper maintenance, your ferret's teeth eventually will need a professional cleaning.

Have your veterinarian perform regular dental exams. Routine cleaning is an effective means of preventive health care. Not only can your vet clean your ferret's teeth, but she also will know what else to look for, such as cracked or broken teeth or indications of a gum abscess. Also, if your ferret is having a problem with his bite or finds chewing painful, he will be unable to eat and may become malnourished. A deep cleaning is usually done under a general anaesthetic, so your pet won't have to be nervous about the procedure.

Having your vet clean your ferret's teeth is important, but you can be proactive as well by making dental care part of your regular grooming routine. Doing so can prevent dental problems down the road. Regular brushing gives you a chance to spot any developing issues early. It will also cut down on the number of professional cleaning visits you will need to make.

How to Brush Your Ferret's Teeth

To brush your ferret's teeth, use a child's toothbrush; a toothbrush meant for cats that consists of a set of short bristles on a rubber tube that fits over your finger; or a piece of gauze wrapped around your finger. To make

Ferrets require little to maintain a tidy appearance.

brushing more agreeable to him, place a dab of his favourite liquid/gel vitamin supplement on the brushing tool. (Never use human toothpaste.) Simply wipe the teeth with the brush or gauze. Aim for cleaning the outside surfaces and gums first, paying particular attention to the gum line. Then, if your ferret hasn't become terribly impatient, clean the other surfaces as well.

As with many other grooming procedures, your ferret may object strenuously at first, but if you are patient and gently persist, slowly increasing the amount of teeth that you brush, chances are he will come to accept tooth brushing as part of his

normal routine. Try to brush the teeth at least once a week.

Grooming as Bonding Time

There is no better way to spend quality time with your ferret than during grooming. With each session, your ferret should start to feel more relaxed and become accustomed to being handled by you, which soon will become second nature to him. Grooming also provides a quiet moment during which your ferret can grow to trust you and enjoy your company, making your bond grow even stronger.

Showing Your Ferret

Ferret shows are hosted by clubs and organisations throughout the UK. They are also held in the US, Japan, and Australia. These events offer ferret fanciers an opportunity to enter their pets in competition to see how well they match up to the conformation standard for the breed in the eyes of official judges.

Shows are an excellent way of educating the public about ferrets and providing educational information to owners about the proper care and maintenance of their pets. They are for everyone, not just for breeders or animals that were acquired from breeders. The ferret that you bought at the pet shop or adopted from a shelter has the same chance of taking home the first prize as any other animal being shown. There are no prerequisites to qualifying, so anyone can enter.

Show ferrets must be in top form for competition, however. They must be well groomed and have friendly temperaments so that the judges can do what they need to during the judging. Show ferrets must also be accustomed to being handled by strangers because the judges will be picking them up and checking them out from head to tail as they are being evaluated.

Some shows have fun events such as a "best dressed ferrets" competition. The best part of attending a show is that you get to hobnob with other enthusiasts and can exchange important and useful information.

To find out more about showing your ferret, visit the British Ferret Club website at www.britishferretclub.co.uk or The National Ferret Welfare Association website at www. nfws.net.

Chapter 5

Feeling Good

Keeping your ferret healthy requires constant attention to his daily needs, as well as sensitivity to his normal behaviours and reactions to the environment in which he lives. If you familiarise yourself with his routines, play behaviour, feeding habits, and basic social interactions, you will know when something is bothering him. A loving owner will, of course, want to provide the best care possible to ensure a healthy and long life for her beloved companion.

Naturally, all pets get sick from time to time, but preventing your ferret from becoming ill is much easier than treating him after the fact. An important aspect of his health management is the care you provide on a daily basis. Part of that responsibility is locating a veterinarian who can evaluate your pet soon after you bring him home. During the initial visit, you can make sure that he receives all necessary vaccinations and have him screened for possible common ailments. Also, regularly monitoring your ferret's condition by having him receive an annual wellness exam will ensure his well-being and add to his longevity.

Finding a Vet

The following may seem like a lot of work to go through to find a veterinarian, but your ferret's well-being depends upon finding the most experienced professional care available. Try to choose a vet who is experienced in ferret medicine and who sees them regularly in her practice.

Starting Your Search

Begin researching a vet *before* you have an emergency.

• Check the British Ferret Club at www.britishferretclub.co.uk and National Ferret Welfare Association at www.nfws.net.to see if there are any listed in your area who specialise in ferrets.

• Next, ask your breeder or any other ferret keepers you know where they take their animals. If you don't have this option, check the yellow pages for veterinarians who specialise in exotic animals (these include ferrets, rabbits, and rodents).

• Another option I have included in my search is to select a few veterinarians who do *not* advertise as avian or exotic. I phone and ask who they refer their clients to if they have a serious ferret case.

Your ferret is dependent on you for his good health and well-being.

At this point, you should have several possibilities from which to choose. The next step is to phone each veterinarian's practice and let the receptionist know that you are concerned with finding the very best veterinary care possible for your ferret. Ask if you can arrange to speak directly to the vet at her convenience. Leave both your work and home phone numbers and specific times that the veterinarian can reach you, or ask when it may be a good time for you to call back.

Screening Questions

When you speak with each vet, be prepared to discuss the concerns you may have, and be sure to get all of your questions answered. Here are some good things to ask:

- How many ferrets are seen at the clinic each week?

- Has the vet owned ferrets as personal pets?

- How many ferrets are neutered each week?

- How many ferrets are treated for adrenal disease each week? (This disease is prevalent in ferrets by age 5.)

- Does food have to be removed the night before surgery? (The answer should be "no." Ferrets can wait to be fasted the morning of the procedure.)

- To get an idea if the vet is up to date on the latest advances in the field, you might also want to ask if she regularly attends veterinary

FAMILY-FRIENDLY TIP

Preparing for a Vet Visit

Visiting vets—even ferret vets—can be scary, but it can be a valuable opportunity for children to learn about responsible pet care. Make the trip to the veterinarian a pleasant experience for both your ferret and your child. Explain that pets need checkups to stay healthy, just like everyone else in the family. Also, because the ferret cannot tell you where he hurts, it's up to the vet to figure out what may be making him sick.

Knowing in advance what will occur during the visit is helpful, especially if children realise that the vet will perform many of the same procedures their vet does, such as look inside the ears, listen to the heart, examine the eyes, and palpate the belly. They should understand that the ferret is not being hurt during the exam, but he may be a little nervous, which is normal. A vet visit also gives them an opportunity to ask questions so that they can learn more about how to properly care for their pet.

Feeling Good

conferences about ferret medicine.

- What are the clinic's regular hours? Does it offer night and weekend appointments?
- Is there a vet on call in case of an after-hours emergency? (If not, what does the clinic recommend that you do with your pet?)
- What are the fees for practice visits and vaccinations?
- What are the payment options?

If you don't get the answers you want, continue your search until you find a vet who seems competent and reliable.

Do not make your choice based on how close the veterinarian is to your home (unless that veterinarian is your first choice). Placing your ferret's care in the hands of a vet who does not know anything (or very little) about ferrets isn't the best alternative and could cost the life of your companion. Also, don't assume that just because a vet works with other small companion pets that she is experienced with the special needs of ferrets, especially older ferrets.

The Vet Visit

An annual veterinary checkup is a prerequisite to your ferret's continued good health and longevity. It allows the vet to monitor his overall condition, as well as alert her to any potential health problems. During the checkup, your pet will get a complete examination and receive updates on vaccinations or medications. His vital organs will be checked, and he will be inspected for

Pet Insurance

Many owners purchase pet insurance for their animals. Pet health insurance companies write policies that work like human health insurance does. The owner pays a monthly or annual premium and submits claims as she incurs vet bills. After fulfilling the deductible requirements (which vary based on the policy and the amount of coverage), the owner is reimbursed for a percentage of her expenses.

Before buying a policy, research the insurance company (to make sure they're legitimate and have a reliable reputation) and read the policy carefully so that you know what you're buying. It should explicitly state what veterinary services (such as spaying/neutering, dental care, lab costs, vaccinations, or emergency treatments) and procedures are covered and which ones aren't.

If you're interested in buying a policy for your ferret, ask your vet to recommend a reputable agency that specialises in this type of insurance.

fleas, worms, or other parasites, and examined for lumps or growths. The vet will check his teeth, weight, and temperature. Sometimes she will ask for a stool sample or draw blood for tests. This is a good time for you to ask any questions that you have about your ferret's diet or to mention specific concerns that you have about his health.

Vaccinations

In the United Kingdom no vaccinations are requird for ferrets. However, some owners do vaccinate against canine distemper, which is nearly always fatal in ferrets.

Please check with your veterinarian the suitability of vaccinating your ferret.

Not all vets treat ferrets, so be sure to select an exotic animal specialist who will know how to care for your pet.

Vaccine Reactions

Like other animals, ferrets occasionally have adverse reactions to vaccinations, typically on the second or third exposure to a particular vaccine. Reactions are rare, but these reactions can be life-threatening.

There are several kinds of reactions you should be alert to and prepared to deal with. The most dangerous, an anaphylactic response, usually occurs within an hour after receiving the vaccination. For this reason, you may want to stay at your vet's practice for 30 to 60 minutes afterward, just in case your ferret needs intervention.

Once home, watch for vomiting, diarrhoea, or loss of bladder/bowel control; signs of nausea or dizziness; dark bluish-purple blotches spreading under the skin; difficulty breathing; pale or bright pink gums, ears, feet, or nose; seizures, convulsions, or passing out; or anything else that's alarming.

Bad reactions are hard to miss. Get your ferret back to the vet right away. She will probably administer a shot of antihistamine (Benadryl) and perhaps a corticosteroid or epinephrine. Ferrets who have had mild to moderate anaphylactic reactions to a particular vaccine can be pretreated with an antihistamine the next time, or you might consider switching to a different vaccine. If your ferret has had a severe reaction, you and your vet can discuss the relative dangers of leaving him unvaccinated.

Most delayed reactions aren't dangerous. You might notice your ferret acting tired, showing flu-like symptoms, or possibly even vomiting a little within a day or two after getting the vaccination. As long as the symptoms don't last longer than a day and don't seem too extreme, there's no need to worry. If your ferret has trouble breathing, is more than a little lethargic, or shows other worrisome symptoms, call or visit your vet right away. Antihistamines don't help much with delayed reactions, but your vet might suggest pretreating your pet next time in the event that it may help.

Signs of Illness

Knowing the warning signs of illness can help you help your ferret sooner, which may prevent him from becoming seriously ill, and in some cases, can save his life. Besides, preventing him from unnecessary pain or suffering is always better than trying to treat him after the fact.

To recognise the onset of illness in your ferret, you must know what to look for. There are a number of telltale signs that indicate it may be a good idea to get your pet to the vet sooner rather than later.

Physical Changes

- black debris in or around the ears
- difficulty breathing or laboured breathing
- distended belly (large belly out of proportion to the rest of the body)
- hair loss, especially on the base of the tail by the rump, at the shoulders, on the tops of the feet, or on the top of the head
- injuries or scabs
- lumps or bumps
- rear-end or generalised weakness
- red, bleeding, or sensitive gums
- unusually smelly ears
- weight loss (except during seasonal

A Healthy Ferret Checklist

A healthy ferret should be:
- playful, alert, and interactive with you
- curious with a gentle nature

and have:
- a slightly elongated body, muscular but not bony
- a full, soft, shiny coat
- bright eyes with little or no discharge
- clean ears and a moist nose
- healthy teeth and pink gums

coat changes)
- winking or squinting with one eye

Behavioural Changes

- aggression toward other ferrets when they usually get along
- coughing
- excessive itchiness or scratching
- grinding teeth
- lying down every few steps
- pawing at the mouth
- playing less than usual
- sexual behaviour (mounting) in neutered males
- sleeping more than usual

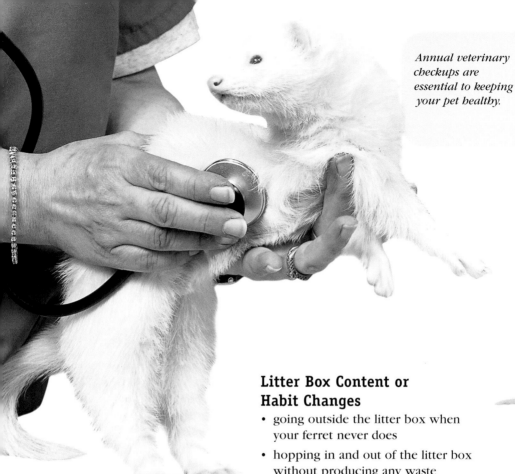

Annual veterinary checkups are essential to keeping your pet healthy.

• staring off into space

• vomiting

Appetite Changes

• being finicky about foods he usually likes

• drinking more than usual

• eating less than usual

• not taking treats he loves

Litter Box Content or Habit Changes

• going outside the litter box when your ferret never does

• hopping in and out of the litter box without producing any waste

• toileting in food dishes or on beds/blankets

• runny, green, or "seedy" waste that occurs several times in a row

• straining to defecate or urinate

General Illnesses

Ferrets are prone to a variety of health problems. If you learn how to spot specific symptoms, you will be able to "ferret out" potential illnesses before they become untreatable or require

When Veterinary Intervention Is a Must

Ferrets are active, curious, and mischievous animals. Sometimes, though, their adventures could land them in a bit of trouble, and they may end up in a situation that requires emergency medical care. If your ferret exhibits any of these conditions, take him to the vet immediately:

Back Leg Weakness: If your ferret is dragging one or both back legs, this may indicate low blood sugar, insulinoma, or neurological trauma.

Dehydration: A ferret's skin should rebound quickly after a gentle pinch. Skin that rebounds slowly indicates that the animal is dehydrated. Dehydration also may indicate kidney disease.

Diarrhoea: Diarrhoea is a symptom of viral or bacterial infection. If bright green, it indicates ECE (green slime virus), in which case you should contact your vet immediately.

Lethargy or Loss of Appetite: Sluggishness or lack of appetite can be a warning sign of various illnesses, including severe infection, insulinoma, adrenal disease, or kidney disease. Tiring quickly while playing may be a symptom of heart disease. Weight loss can indicate kidney disease or lymphosarcoma.

Loss of Hair: Hair loss along the back, tail, and rump that is not associated with shedding indicates adrenal tumours. Hair loss also may result from external parasites or a low-quality diet.

Pale Gums: Gums should appear pink and healthy. To test, apply gentle pressure to the gums. They should rapidly return to pink. Pale gums may indicate anaemia, shock, septicaemia, or a heart condition.

Rapid or Difficult Breathing: Rapid breathing is a warning sign of heart disease, while difficulty breathing is a symptom of lymphosarcoma.

Vomiting: Gagging or vomiting are symptomatic of a variety of problems, ranging from hairballs or swallowing an indigestible object to ulcers, liver disease, kidney disease, or insulinoma.

more invasive treatment. Most are treatable if caught early enough.

Abscesses: Abscesses are an accumulation of pus surrounded by infected tissue and usually occur as the result of a puncture or bite wound. Other types of abscesses include dental abscesses and mastitis (infection of the mammary glands). Treatment involves drainage or lancing, cleaning, and a suitable broad spectrum antibiotic.

Anaemia: Anaemia is caused by a deficiency of red blood cells. The three most common causes of anaemia in ferrets are heavy flea infestation, lymphoma tumours, and oestrogen toxicity in intact females. Treatment includes blood transfusion from a ferret donor.

Canine Distemper: Distemper is a highly contagious viral disease. It is transmitted directly from one infected animal to another. Clinical signs include mild conjunctivitis, fever, and purulent nasal discharge. Ferrets develop a pattern of thickening and crusting of the skin around the chin, lips, and footpads. There is no treatment for this disease.

Coccidiosis: This parasite is found most frequently in immature animals and may cause severe diarrhoea and dehydration. It is usually due to

poor sanitation and can be picked up from the environment. Treatment includes the use of sulfa-based antibiotics.

Dental Disease: Dental tartar and periodontal disease are common. Regular teeth brushing will help to prevent dental disease.

Ear Mites: Ferrets naturally have dark brown earwax in their ear canals. Because wax can often build up, their ears need regular cleaning. However, if you notice your ferret scratching his ears, he may have ear mites, so take him to the vet for treatment. If he is diagnosed with ear mites, thoroughly clean the cage and bedding.

Eosinophilic Gastroenteritis: Eosinophilic gastroenteritis is an intestinal disordered by the abnormal accumulation of white blood cells in the intestinal wall and associated lymph nodes. This is a syndrome of unknown cause. Clinical signs include intermittent vomiting, loss of appetite, diarrhoea, and weight loss. Treatment includes nutritional support and corticosteroids.

Fleas: Fleas are external parasites that bite the skin and suck their host's blood. Because they can cause serious health problems such as anaemia, make every effort to eliminate them. If you have cats or dogs who go outside, they may carry fleas back into the house in temperate seasons. If your ferret is allowed to play in the same areas as your other pets, he will become infested quickly. Pyrethrins, chemicals that are relatively safe even on baby kits, act as flea repellents and kill adult fleas. Products containing pyrethrins are available in many forms, including powders, sprays, and towelettes that can be wiped over the animal.

Gastric and Duodenal Ulcers: Gastric and duodenal ulcers, sores on the lining of the digestive tract, can occur in ferrets. The underlying cause is not known, although environmental stress may be a predisposing factor. Signs include loss of appetite, vomiting, hypersalivation, tooth grinding, and blood in the stool. Diagnosis is by X-ray, endoscopy, and/or exploratory surgery and biopsy.

The best way to treat ulcers in ferrets is to prevent them before they start. Overcrowding, poor sanitation,

introduction of new animals into an established group, and rearrangement of the normal social order are all factors that commonly cause an increase in stress and the incidence of gastric ulcers.

Heartworm Disease: Heartworms are not found in the UK. However, if you are taking your ferret abroad you will need to discuss a preventative with your veterinarian. Heartworms are parasites that affect the heart adversely. Prevention is imperative. In ferrets, the disease resembles the canine form. However, because of the ferret's small size, the presence of only one adult worm may be fatal. Heartworm is transmitted by the mosquito when it bites its host. Both indoor and outdoor animals can become infected. In ferrets, heartworm is usually not detected until cardiac failure occurs. Signs include difficulty breathing, fluid buildup in the abdomen, heart murmur, and loss

of appetite. Diagnosis is difficult. X-rays of the chest may help to diagnose the disease, as may blood tests. Treatment is also difficult, so a preventive medication is your best bet.

Heatstroke:

Ferrets do not have well-developed sweat glands and so are prone to heat exhaustion. Clinical signs include panting and flaccid inactivity. Hot and humid conditions should be minimised by ensuring adequate air circulation and/or cooling in enclosures. Optimum temperatures are 40° to 65°F (4.4° to 18.3°C) with a humidity range of 40 to 65 percent.

Ferrets who are overheated start to breathe through their mouths. As they become even warmer, heatstroke can occur along with the following signs: bright red tongue, coma, depression, diarrhoea, dizziness, rapid panting, red or pale gums, shock, thick and sticky saliva, vomiting (sometimes with blood),

Changes in your pet's behaviour or appearance may indicate that he is ill.

Medical care should be provided at the first sign of illness to ensure the best recovery.

and weakness. Treatment involves lowering your ferret's temperature by submerging his body in lukewarm water while keeping his head elevated above the water. Then, after he has cooled down, place him on a wet towel and seek veterinary attention immediately.

Influenza: Ferrets are susceptible to the same influenza viral strains that affect humans. Generally, it causes only mild illness and discomfort in ferrets. Signs include sneezing with a clear nasal discharge, conjunctivitis, coughing, and fever. Treatment basically involves easing the symptoms and letting the virus run its course. Fluids may be given subcutaneously (under the skin) if dehydration is present. Also, oral electrolyte solutions are helpful.

Ringworm: Ferrets are highly susceptible to ringworm, a fungal skin infection that can be transmitted to and from humans and other pets. It is marked by ring-shaped, reddened, scaly, or blistery patches. Antifungal

Ferret Physiology

- The average life span for a ferret is six to nine years.
- Sexual maturity occurs at five to nine months of age.
- The gestation period is 41 to 42 days.
- A ferret's eyes open between 28 and 37 days.
- The weaning age is six to eight weeks, with eight weeks preferable.
- A ferret's normal body temperature is 100° to 103°F (37.8 to 39.4°C).
- The ferret's gastrointestinal transit time is three to four hours.
- The normal heart rate is 180 to 250 beats per minute.

ointments must be prescribed by a veterinarian and may require application for a month or two.

Ticks: Ticks are skin parasites. Just as with fleas, they can be picked up walking your ferret outside or from other household pets. Although the bites do not always itch, they can be painful and become infected.

To remove a tick, grasp it with tweezers as close to its mouth parts as possible, and pull gently. Make sure that the mouth parts are not left in the skin. Disinfect the area with soap and water or alcohol after tick removal. Never dip a ferret.

Urinary Tract Obstruction: Urethral obstruction in male ferrets may occur secondary to pressure from a cyst around the urinary tract occurring between the bladder and genital. Signs are compatible with urinary tract stones and include straining to urinate, blood in the urine, or inability to urinate. Treatment requires surgical removal of the obstruction.

Urinary Tract Stones: The most common cause of stones in the urinary tract is feeding inappropriate food such as low-quality ferret food, inappropriate dog food, or low-quality cat food. Signs include straining to urinate, blood in the urine, or inability to urinate. Treatment requires surgical removal of the stones.

Ferret-Specific Illnesses

The following are ailments and diseases more commonly associated with ferrets.

Aleutian Disease: Aleutian Disease is the result of an AIDS-like parvovirus that is able to survive on many surfaces and in most temperatures. (Several strains of parvovirus affect both minks and ferrets.) It is a progressive disease affecting various organs of the body. Clinical signs vary, and the incubation period of the disease can be as long as 200 days. Symptoms range from posterior weakness to paralysis, and include dark tarry stools, lethargy, urinary incontinence, and a slow, wasting deterioration of the body. Diagnosis is based on a positive ADV test. There is no treatment.

Adrenal Gland Tumours: Adrenal tumours are common in ferrets, occurring with the same frequency as insulinomas and often concurrently. Signs include bilaterally symmetric hair loss, usually starting at the tail base and progressing up the body. There may be a history of hair loss and spontaneous regrowth. Itching is often reported, as well as skin dryness. Loss of muscle tone and weakness may be present, along with an enlarged vulva in females. Treatment involves surgically removing the tumour.

Medicinal treatment of adrenal disease is usually reserved for ferrets who are poor surgical candidates. They may be older ferrets or ferrets with other medical problems that would make surgery high risk. The two drugs used most frequently and successfully for the treatment of adrenal disease are Lupron and Melatonin. Neither will cure the disease, but they may provide relief of the symptoms.

Cardiomyopathy: Cardiomyopathy is an enlargement of the heart that most frequently affects ferrets over two years old. There are two forms: hypertrophic and dilated. Hypertrophic is a thickening of the heart muscle, causing a decreased size of the chambers of the heart. Dilated is a loss of muscle tone that decreases the strength of the heart muscle. Therefore, the heart cannot pump blood.

Symptoms include a heart murmur, weight loss, decreased activity, and difficulty breathing. Treatment depends on the type diagnosed. Diagnosis is obtained by X-ray and ultrasound. Treatment for dilated is aimed at increasing heart muscle strength, increasing normal heart function, and reducing fluid accumulation. Treatment for hypertrophic consists of calcium channel blockers, beta blockers, diuretics, and ACE inhibitors.

Disseminated Idiopathic Myositis (DIM): First defined in 2003 in the United States, DIM appears to be a new disease in ferrets. The cause is unknown. Usually, it results in a fatal inflammatory condition of the

Many diseases common to ferrets are treatable if caught early.

muscles called "myositis." Physical signs include high fever, tiredness, weakness, reluctance to move, pain with handling (over the back or hips), decreased appetite, increased respiratory and heart rates, clear nasal discharge, and enlarged lymph nodes in the leg(s) or neck area. There is currently no known definitive treatment for DIM.

Endocrine Tail Alopecia: The cause of ferret tail hair loss is unknown. It is suspected to be due to hormonal fluctuations because the disease responds to changes in the photoperiod. Many nutritional, medical, and dermatological remedies have been tried. Sometimes the hair grows back with or without treatment. Usually, when the ferret changes his coat in the fall, the tail hair regrows, but he is likely to lose it again the next spring.

Epizootic Catarrhal Enteritis (ECE): ECE is a ferret-specific disease that damages the intestinal lining with inflammation and infection. When the intestinal lining is damaged, the ferret has difficulty absorbing nutrients and water into his body. This results in

diarrhoea, excess mucus production, and dehydration. In severe cases, intestinal ulceration and bleeding take place. ECE has been identified as a virus, not a bacterial infection. The disease also is known as the "greenies" or "green slime disease."

ECE is characterised by the sudden onset of profuse, watery, bright green diarrhoea (although the diarrhoea also can be other shades of green or yellow). It is often accompanied by vomiting (in the early stages of the disease), lethargy, diminished eating or drinking, or refusal to eat or drink altogether.

Treatment is directed toward supportive care of the affected animal, such as keeping him hydrated and nourished. He should be given fluids and nutrition. Also, by administering antibiotics, secondary bacterial infections can be prevented.

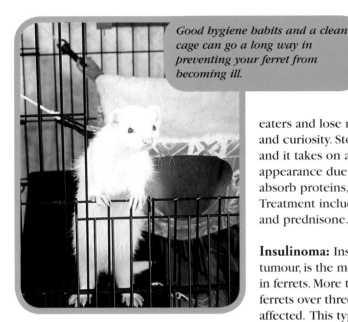

Good hygiene habits and a clean cage can go a long way in preventing your ferret from becoming ill.

Helicobacter Infection: *Helicobacter mustelae* is extremely widespread in ferrets. Several studies have shown that almost every ferret carries this bacteria. Because it is passed through a faecal–oral route, kits generally are infected by their mother within the first two weeks of life. Few symptoms other than intermittent tarry faeces have been attributed to Helicobacter infections. Treatment includes a triple therapy of amoxicillin, Flagyl, and Pepto-Bismol.

Inflammatory Bowel Disease (IBD): Inflammatory bowel disease is a chronic condition that occurs in many animal species, including people. IBD is the result of the body fighting a foreign substance in the GI tract. Ferrets normally have a rather loose stool, so the early signs of mucoid and watery stools may be overlooked until the condition is rather advanced. Ferrets with IBD become picky eaters and lose much of their energy and curiosity. Stool frequency increases, and it takes on a grainy "bird seed" appearance due to an inability to absorb proteins, fats, and carbohydrates. Treatment includes amoxicillin, Flagyl, and prednisone.

Insulinoma: Insulinoma, or a pancreatic tumour, is the most common tumour in ferrets. More than 30 percent of ferrets over three years of age are affected. This type of tumour causes low blood sugar. Symptoms include depression, "stargazing" (staring into space), posterior weakness, and seizures. The most telling signs include profuse salivation and pawing at the mouth, which are indicative of nausea. Treatment includes surgery to debulk the tumour—this is only a temporary treatment, though. Treatment also includes frequent feeding and administering prednisone and dizoxide as necessary.

Lymphosarcoma: Lymphosarcoma (lymphoma) is a malignant cancer that involves the lymphoid system. It is common in ferrets. The most commonly affected organs are the spleen, liver, and lymph nodes of the chest and extremities. Clinical signs are dependent upon the organs affected. They include weight loss,

usually appearing on the tail. This is due to an overproduction of sebum in the body. These blackheads usually can be cleared up by shampooing with antiseborrheic shampoos (usually available from the veterinarian). These special shampoos may contain benzoyl peroxide or salicylic acid, and they are most effective when left on the skin for several minutes before rinsing.

enlarged spleen, lethargy, difficulty breathing, enlarged lymph nodes, and skin tumours. Treatment may include surgery and/or chemotherapy.

Mast Cell Tumours: Mast cell tumours are the most common skin tumours in ferrets and are often benign. They appear as individual tumours that are slightly raised, flat, button-like masses. Treatment involves surgical removal and biopsy.

Posterior Paralysis: Posterior paralysis or hind limb weakness is a common symptom associated with many diseases, and it is necessary to work with your veterinarian to determine the cause, and hopefully, treatment, for the underlying condition.

Tail Blackheads: Another common skin ailment in ferrets is blackheads,

Seasonal Changes

Ferrets have dramatic seasonal changes in the length, thickness, and colour of their coat, a normal occurrence that is triggered by the change of the seasons. Coats generally get shorter and darker coloured in the summer months and longer, thicker, and lighter in colour in the winter.

Stress

Reducing stress might not have a direct effect on any specific disease, but a ferret who is not stressed will have better overall health and may do better if he gets sick. There are several things you can do to reduce the overall stress levels in your ferret's daily life and in his environment.

Change: Change in and of itself isn't necessarily stressful—some amount of change actually helps to mentally stimulate your ferrets. However, other types of change can be anxiety provoking (introduction of new ferrets, loss of a cagemate, change in daily routine, etc.). Even excitement can be stressful: Positive change can cause stress as much as negative change. Whenever possible, implement change gradually.

Darkness: Ferrets are descended from burrowing animals, and burrows are dark. If your ferret does not have a dark place to go to when he's tired, frightened, or just not feeling well, he may become stressed. Provide a dark area for him, such as a nest box or sleep sack in his cage, which will give him a sense of security and calm.

Death: Losing a ferret can be hard on your other ferrets as well as on you. Like people, some will just go on with their lives. Others may sink into a deep depression, but most fall somewhere in between. The most difficult problems

seem to occur when a ferret in a strongly bonded pair dies.

Illness: Serious illness causes stress on the body, but even a brief minor illness can be stressful both physically and mentally. But the stress may not be limited to the animal who is ill; the other ferrets in the group also may be affected. Pay extra attention to how all the ferrets in your group are behaving whenever you have an ill ferret in your home, and act accordingly.

Loneliness: Ferrets like company. If your ferret is an only ferret, make sure you spend a lot of time with him.

Better yet, consider getting him a companion.

New Ferrets: Adding a new ferret to your group can be stressful for everyone. Gradual introductions in which you allow the ferrets to get acquainted slowly before housing them together will help them get used to one another. You'll have to allow them to work things out on their own for the most part. Although there will be some dragging around, hissing, and squabbling, your ferrets will work things out.

Noise: Loud noises can frighten ferrets. Things like vacuum cleaners, appliances, lawn mowers, and loud

The Importance of Ferret-Specific Care

The best first aid a ferret can have is a knowledgeable owner and a veterinarian well versed in the latest ferret care. Being proactive instead of reactive to your pet's health is the first step to ensuring good health and longevity.

The biggest problem ferret owners face is that most veterinarians do not know much about ferret care. Providing treatment as if your ferret were a cat or a dog can, more often than not, have a negative outcome, and your ferret may pay the price. As a responsible owner, you must have adequate knowledge and basic skills to care for your ferret. Speaking from experience, there will be times when you need to know more than the vet. Be prepared! Also, most 24-hour clinics know nothing about ferrets. Count on Murphy's Law: Your ferret *will* get sick in the middle of the night or over a weekend when your ferret-knowledgeable vet is not available.

Being trained and prepared in basic supportive care can make the difference until you can get to your own vet. Have an emergency plan in place before the emergency happens. Know where the emergency clinics are and how to get there. Keep the numbers in a prominent place.

Ferret First-Aid Kit

In the event of an emergency, it's a good idea to have a ferret-appropriate first-aid kit at your disposal. Besides contact info for your vet, here's what should be in it:

- 1 cc oral and tuberculin syringes
- 1–2 tins of high-quality dry food
- 1–2 jars chicken or turkey baby food
- alcohol wipes
- butterfly needle sets
- clean towel
- cold pack
- cornflour/styptic powder
- cotton balls
- cotton-tipped applicators
- first-aid tape
- gauze pads
- heating beds (not electric)
- hot water bottle
- hydrogen peroxide

- iodine
- isolation/hospital cage
- magnifying glass
- electrolyte replacer
- petroleum jelly
- puppy pads, bed pads
- rectal thermometer
- rubbing alcohol
- scissors
- self-adhering bandage material
- small bottle of Karo syrup
- triple antibiotic ointment
- tweezers
- vet wrap (optional)

music, all can create stress. Place their housing in peaceful areas of the house so that they have a secure place to retreat to when necessary.

Play: Ferrets are active animals. They need frequent physical stimulation and regular exercise. Play is not just for their body—it's also for their mind. Spend quality time with your pet every day. You can simply toss around a toy, or you can teach your ferret tricks. Any kind of interaction with you will be valuable.

Travel: Ferrets generally travel well. But changing their surroundings, especially for an ill ferret going to the veterinarian, can cause stress. When preparing a travel carrier, make sure

that you include things that smell like home. Take a blanket or sleep sack that your ferret normally uses so that the enclosure feels familiar to him. For long trips, make sure that you bring water from home. Some areas of the country have more or less chlorine in the water, which can affect your ferret's digestion.

Senior Ferret Care

Ferrets have an average life span of 6 to 9 years, with some living 10 years or longer. However, some may begin to experience problems associated with midlife as early as 3 to 4 years of age. More frequent checkups, about every 6 months, are recommended for older ferrets. Seniors can develop illnesses rapidly, especially cancer, kidney, and heart disease. Waiting an entire year

Care of a Sick Ferret

Taking proper care of a sick ferret can aid in his recovery and can even help him heal more quickly. Always keep a sick pet in a warm, quiet area and monitor his water and food intake. Inform your veterinarian if he is constipated or has diarrhoea for a prolonged period. Carefully administer any prescribed medications. Do not attempt to treat your ferret with human medications or antibiotics bought at a pet shop. Many of these medications may be poisonous to ferrets at improper dosages and could harm or kill your pet. During treatment, it might be necessary to quarantine a sick ferret from any other ferrets you have, especially if the ailment is contagious or your sick ferret needs quiet rest. Your vet will let you know whether this is required.

After any kind of surgery, make sure your ferret's cage remains clean to prevent any secondary bacterial infections of the surgery site. Check the incision each day for swelling or discharge. Also monitor whether your ferret is chewing the stitches. Be sure to consult with your vet if your ferret has not eaten or defecated within 24 hours after returning home.

between visits could prevent the early detection and management of these diseases.

Starting at four years of age laboratory work is usually recommended. Even if your ferret appears healthy, a complete blood cell count and a fasting blood glucose should be obtained. This routine lab work should be done once a year. Additional lab work, a blood chemistry profile, and an X-ray, particularly if the ferret is exhibiting signs of illness, are recommended.

After the age of 6, diagnostic testing should be done every 6 months along with a bi-annual examination. These laboratory workups are invaluable in detecting many diseases early and thus facilitating early treatment.

Healthy older ferrets tend to stay playful and energetic, but owners should learn to recognise the signs of ageing and know how to adjust their daily care to their changing needs. For example, seniors require more rest and sleep, they may have more difficulty with eating or proper toileting, or their normal activities may become limited due to pain, illness, or just old age. By creating a proper diet, encouraging regular exercise, and providing appropriate health care, you will ensure the best life possible for your pet throughout his golden years.

Chapter 6

Being Good

Ferrets are full of boundless energy. They will entertain you for hours. While you work on training them, they will be working on training you. Just remember that ferrets begin to mature at six months of age, so forget the cuddling until then. Your young ferret is going to want to play and explore, and he won't like being restrained.

I f your ferret is older, he will probably not be rambunctious, but he will be just as much fun. Mature ferrets slow down a bit, but they are still just as lovable and curious. In fact, one of the joys of ferret ownership is that, unlike mature cats and dogs, ferrets never lose their playfulness. No matter how old they are, ferrets want and need lots of love and companionship.

Bonding is a process that will require time, nurturing, and plenty of patience. Consider the first month to be a critical time for your new pet. He will have to adapt to his new environment. Shy or nervous ferrets need extra time. It is crucial to allow your pet to adapt at his own speed.

Well worth the effort, proper handling and careful training will enhance the bond that you share. Just be sure to make the experience fun for both of you.

Proper Handling

A ferret who has happily adjusted to a home with his human family loves to be cuddled and petted. To ensure that your ferret becomes tame and accepts human contact, handle him frequently and correctly every day. Picking him up improperly could permanently frighten him and make him fearful and aggressive.

If you have just brought home a new ferret, your first instinct may be to take him out of his cage to play—don't! Let his first few days at home be quiet ones. Allow him to adapt to his cage environment. It is important for him

FAMILY-FRIENDLY TIP

Involving a Child in Training

Do not buy a ferret (or any pet) to teach a child responsibility; instead, buy a ferret for a responsible child. Remember, once you have learned how to handle a ferret properly, it is crucial that you teach your children how to handle and treat him properly as well. Rough handling can cause an animal to become frightened and bite, which is something you want to avoid. In general, young children always should be supervised when holding or playing with pets. A child's age and maturity level will determine when handling is appropriate. Once a child is capable of holding her pet comfortably, she can begin having fun teaching him tricks.

to first feel secure in his own space. Your best course of action is to let him investigate his cage, including the litter box. Begin with short handling sessions, then increase the duration as he feels more comfortable.

Because ferrets have limited vision, always speak to your pet in a gentle tone of voice before you pick him up. This will not only let him know you are approaching but will let him become familiar with your voice and his name.

When picking up your ferret, always lift him from behind using two hands: one supporting his chest, the other cradling his hips. Then, gently lift him and hold him against your chest. Never pick up your ferret by his tail or grab him unexpectedly. Be careful not to make any sudden movements toward him; he may be nervous and nip if you do. Let the little one come to you. He will let you know when he wants to be picked up by holding onto your leg or grabbing your wrist when you extend your hand.

Socialisation

Socialisation does not come easily to some pets, and sometimes it is hard to imagine that it will ever come at all. Some antisocial behaviour is normal for a pet who is unfamiliar with his environment or to an animal who has had you or his domain all to himself.

At first, a great deal of the interaction between you and your new ferret (or your ferret and another pet) will likely take the form of hissing, neck grabbing, nipping, or scratching. Until you become friends, there may be a lot of what appears to be thoughtless and unkind behaviour. A more aggressive pet will try to establish dominance over the more submissive one. Your ferret may be timid and defensive for a bit, but eventually, with your help, he will be confidently scampering about feeling like part of the family.

Ferrets With Ferrets

Ferrets who live in harmony with each other willingly share their cage, food, litter box, toys, and human companions. As valuable as a playmate can be, compatibility will depend on the personality, energy level, and age of each ferret.

The advantage of purchasing two kits who already have been cagemates is that these furry friends can develop a strong bond between them. Of course, having two kits means twice the attention, training, and constant supervision. However, I've found that two ferrets really aren't harder to socialise than just one.

When considering a playmate for an older ferret, visit a ferret breeder (who usually has neutered retired breeder animals) or adopt from a

Proper handling and careful training will enhance the bond that you share with your pet.

ferret shelter. Mature ferrets usually have outgrown their pesky adolescent stage. They share the same energy levels as youngsters and are not usually interested in getting into trouble or throwing temper tantrums.

Your new ferret will need to visit the vet for a checkup He also should be tested for Aleutian Disease. Until then, restrict his access to other pets and people, and keep him inside your home. Once he has been given a clean bill of health and has adapted to you and his new environment, you may begin the introduction process.

The first encounter should begin by placing the ferrets' cages side by

No Play Dates, Please!

Animals your ferret will never be friends with:

- birds
- gerbils
- guinea pigs
- hamsters
- mice
- rabbits
- rats
- reptiles

If you have any of these pets in your home, proceed with caution where your ferret is concerned.

Introduce pets to each other gradually so that they have time to get acquainted.

side. In this way, they have an opportunity to become acquainted safely through the cages. There may be a few spats because ferrets can be territorial.

Keep the ferrets separate for a few days. When you feel the time is right, open both cage doors, stand back, and let them come out. They probably will sniff each other from nose to tail, which is normal, then either get along, wrestle a bit, or fight. Allow the initial contact to last for a few minutes. Do not push togetherness. Extend their social time slowly each day until they get used to each other.

Get-acquainted sessions should be brief and scheduled twice a day until the ferrets decide to become roommates. You will know that they are ready when you see them cuddle together in their chosen cage. Friendship takes time; some ferrets bond immediately, some within two to three months, and unfortunately, some never bond. If your ferrets do not bond after six months, separate housing and playtime will be necessary.

Ferrets, Cats, and Dogs

As social animals, most ferrets enjoy meeting new people and other animals. While some owners may fear that their ferret will either harm or be harmed by other family pets, they will likely become playmates or at least civil housemates if you handle

introductions correctly.

In general, cats and ferrets can live harmoniously together. Either your cat will accept the ferret or just decide to avoid him. On occasion, cats have been known to injure a ferret and vice versa, so constant supervision is necessary whenever pets are roaming about at the same time. Puppies and adult dogs tend to tolerate ferrets as well. However, because of their natural instinct, dogs originally bred for hunting may harm or kill your ferret. It is important that dogs living with ferrets be obedience trained, and of course, have constant supervision. Neutered animals usually are less aggressive, gentler, and easier to train.

When you feel that it is time for your cat or dog to meet your ferret, hold the ferret in your lap and keep your other pet on a lead. Be prepared to protect his face and body from a scratch or bite. No matter how gentle or sweet, all animals can become territorial. Only you can determine when it is safe to allow your cat or

Being Good

dog freedom to investigate the ferret off lead. Once your pets become friendly, never allow them to be together unsupervised, regardless of how well they get along. Always pay equal attention to all pets to avoid any jealousy issues from taking hold. With time and patience, you will eventually be one big happy family.

Tricks

Although ferrets are fast learners, tricks are difficult for them because they have a very short attention span. That said, you still can teach them some simple commands. They can learn *come, roll over, roll over and pray, stay,* and *lie down*. Training your ferret can be fun, and it certainly is a great way to spend quality time while strengthening your relationship.

Exercise and playtime out of the cage are essential to your ferret's physical and mental health.

Let your ferret learn one trick before moving on to the next. Remember that this should be fun for both you and your pet. Never use force, harsh corrections, or make your ferret do anything when he's tired. Keep sessions short, and offer lots of praise and affection. It's usually best to start training your ferret when he's young so that he will learn quicker. Ferrets are very intelligent animals who love to interact with their humans. Although they are quick learners, they may forget their new tricks or learned behaviours without continued reinforcement through regular practice. But that's a great excuse to have more fun together.

Here are a few tricks to try:

Come

The quickest way to get your ferret to come to you is to use a very loud squeaky toy. Most ferrets will automatically come running after just one squeak. The trick is to get your ferret to come each and every time. To do so, rewards work best—every ferret loves a tasty treat. When your ferret comes to you after hearing the squeak, give him the reward. Practice this over and over: squeak, then reward. Next, practice the same routine, but this time use his name after the squeak and say "Come." Practice this as needed. Be sure to offer only a small bit of something healthy. After some time, offer the treat only on occasion. Eventually, your ferret will come when called without needing the reward.

Ferret Gestures

Ferrets have a wide range of gestures that mean something to other ferrets—and that other species (even cats and humans) can learn to interpret. Recognising ferret body language and behaviour will help you tame and train your pet.

Arch and Shove: One ferret arches his back in a characteristic way and shoves himself sidelong into another. This is one ferret trying to start a fight with another in a situation he is not sure he can win.

Bottle Brush Tail: This gesture is exactly what it sounds like: The tail will fluff out like a big bottle brush. This is usually precipitated by fear. It also can indicate extreme joyous excitement or extreme anger.

Bumper Cars: A ferret flattens himself out into a sort of Formula One racecar shape and rams another with his open mouth. This is a genuine challenge that should not be taken lightly.

Deflate and Stare: This is an expression of aggravated exasperation. The ferret sighs, collapses without moving his legs, and stares as if you weren't even there. You've just spoiled everything.

Ear Licking: This is a disciplinary measure when applied by a mother to her young, but also, just as in cats, a means of placating a more assertive individual.

Splayed Toes: This indicates utter joy. Cats purr, dogs wag their tails, horses roll their eyes, and ferrets splay their toes.

Vibrating Tail: This indicates a sign of nervous anticipation, high thrills, or exasperation. The ferret swishes his tail back and forth very quickly for a couple of seconds. You usually will only see this if the ferret's head is covered, either in a tube, under a blanket, or inside your trouser leg, but a few will do it in the open. Whatever it may be (an object, attention, etc.), your ferret wants it very, very badly!

Weasel War Dance: The ferret bounces backward on all four feet, sometimes dooking, sometimes hissing, sometimes shaking his head from side to side, and sometimes doing all of the above. This is the same as a dog's rump in the air, elbows on the ground gesture; it's an invitation to play.

Roll Over

For more complicated trick training, use a treat like Ferretone, a small piece of meat, or a piece of your ferret's regular food. Show him the treat, and physically place him in the position you want him to be in. For example, lay him on his stomach and roll him over while saying the command "Roll over." Give him the reward after he is in position, and praise him for a job well done. Do this several times a day and be patient. He'll soon be entertaining you with all of his new antics.

Walking on a Lead

Ferrets love to go for walks, and the safest way to take your furry companion outside is to place him in a harness and on a lead specifically designed for ferrets. Including a tag on the harness that shows your pet's name and your telephone number on it is also a good idea.

The harness should be securely strapped around your ferret's neck and body so that you can barely squeeze your pinkie finger through. Be careful not to put the harness on too tightly, though. Never leave a harness on inside a cage or inside your home either; it could get caught on something and cause injury or a fatal accident. It should only be used for taking your ferret outdoors. Here are some important guidelines:

Ferret Vocalisations

Ferrets never cease to entertain with their silly antics and playful behaviour. Aside from body language, they communicate by vocalising. Understanding ferret language will help you know what your pet is thinking or feeling.

- A loud dooking noise (dook, dook, dook) portends great fun and excitement.
- A similar noise, but sharper and more like a "chuck" than a "dook," means that a ferret is looking for something and not finding it.
- A very loud "chuck" that sounds more like a dog's bark is a warning to all comers that a ferret is being pushed too far.
- A hiss is also a warning, though not as strong as a bark. Ferrets also will hiss if you stop playing with them before they are ready to do so.
- A wavering scream means that a ferret is being pounced on by another ferret with whom he has no wish to fight.
- Whenever any of these calls are given in a monotone, it means a ferret is not excited or interested and just wishes to make his opinion known. The more undulation that is added to these calls, the more excited the ferret is becoming.

Instinctually clean and neat, most ferrets can be trained to use a litter box.

- Do not use a harness made from plastic. Ferrets will chew on and swallow plastic, causing gastrointestinal blockage and possible death.

- Never walk your ferret on paved surfaces during hot weather. These hot surfaces will burn his delicate paws. It's not a good idea to take your ferret outside on hot days anyway because he could suffer from dehydration or heatstroke.

- Pick up your ferret when other pets come near.

Training a ferret to wear a harness takes planning and patience:

- Wait until your ferret has played for an hour or so and is starting to get tired.

- Take him to a small, confined area such as a bathroom or bedroom and try to put the harness on. At first, your ferret will probably do everything possible to get it off.

- Leave the harness on for five to ten minutes, supervising him at all times.

- Repeat this procedure daily, extending the time slowly until your ferret finally accepts the harness. You might try a little distraction with a favourite toy.

- Add a lead when your ferret is used to the harness. Hold it securely so

that your pet can roam only as far as you want him to.

- Repeat this procedure with the lead about five minutes each time. Then remove it and put it away until your ferret goes outside with you.

Litter Box Training

When you bring home your ferret, and after he has had the chance to settle in, you will want to address the issue of housetraining. Ferrets are actually very clean and neat. These little animals like to have their bathroom area away from their eating and sleeping areas. They often will choose the corners of their cage and will pick one spot in which to toilet, which they will continue to use. As a result, ferrets can be trained to use a litter tray. The key to success is to let your ferret choose his corner first, then place the litter box or tray in that location.

In the Cage

To begin litter box training your ferret, start him out in a small area, and expand his space gradually as he becomes better trained. If the litter box is in a big cage, you might need to block off part of it at first. Fasten the litter box down so that it can't be tipped over. Keep a little dirty litter in it at first to mark it as a bathroom and to deter your ferret from digging in it. Don't let it get too dirty, though; some ferrets can be pretty finicky about their bathrooms. Most won't mess up their beds or food, so put towels or food bowls in all the other corners until your ferret is used to making the effort to find his box.

Bedding that has been slept in a few times and smells like "sleeping ferret" will be even better than clean bedding for convincing a ferret that a corner is a bedroom instead of a bathroom. Ferrets generally use their boxes within 15 minutes of waking up, so make sure that yours uses the litter box before you let him out, or put him back in the cage five or ten minutes after you wake him up to come out or play. Within a few days, your ferret will probably have caught on and fake using the box just to get out of the cage or to get a treat. That's okay—at least it reinforces the right idea.

During Playtime

When your ferret is out running around during playtime, keep a close eye on him, and put him in his litter box every half hour or so. Whenever he uses a litter box, whether you had to carry

Housetraining Tips

- **Use a low-walled litter box so your ferret can get in and out of it easily.**
- **Leave a little waste in the box to make it clear that it is the toilet area.**
- **Put lots of blankets and towels around the box to clearly separate the bathroom area.**
- **Constantly supervise your ferret while he is out of the cage during the early stages of toilet training.**

him to it or not, give him lots of praise and a little treat right away. Ferrets will do almost anything for treats, and they learn quickly.

Positive reinforcement (using treats and praise) is usually much more effective than any punishment, but if you need one, use a firm "No!" and some cage time. Rubbing your ferret's nose in his mess won't do any good, and it's cruel. He doesn't know it's the wrong place, and ferrets normally sniff their litter boxes anyway. As with all training, consistency and immediacy are crucial. Scolding a ferret for a mistake that's hours or even a few minutes old won't work. If his favourite corner isn't yours, you have a few options. You could put a box in it (or newspaper, if it's a tight spot), or you could place several trays around your home; ferrets have short legs and attention spans, so you'll probably have to do this anyway. Otherwise, try putting a crumpled towel or a food bowl in the well-cleaned corner, making it look more like a bedroom or kitchen than a latrine.

"Accident" corners should be cleaned very well with vinegar, diluted bleach, or another bad-smelling disinfectant (don't let your ferret onto it until it dries!)—specifically so that they don't continue to smell like ferret bathrooms, but also as a general deterrent. For the same reason, you probably shouldn't clean litter boxes with bleach, certainly not the same one you're using as a deterrent elsewhere. Urine that has soaked into wood will still smell like a bathroom to a ferret, even when you can't tell, so be sure to clean it very well. Although almost every ferret can be trained to use a litter box, there is individual variation. Ferrets just aren't as diligent about their boxes as most cats, so there will be an occasional accident.

Even well-trained ferrets tend to lose track of their litter boxes on occasion when they're frightened or excited, or if they're in a new house or room. In general, you can expect at least a 90 percent "hit" rate, although

Quite often, a problem behaviour is the result of something troubling your ferret or causing him discomfort.

Is This Normal?

As unusual as you will find some of your ferret's behaviours, often they are normal traits that are part of his daily routine.

Dreaming: Occasionally, when your ferret is sleeping, you will notice him twitching; this is because he is dreaming. Sometimes ferrets make little dooking or whining noises when they are asleep; this is also a sign of dreaming.

Itching: If your ferret has an itch while sleeping, he will jump out of his hammock like a cat getting a bath to scratch that itch!

Shivering: Ferrets seem to shiver when they wake up from a snooze. This is because their blood lowers in temperature as they sleep. When they eventually wake up, they have to shiver to make their blood temperature go back up again.

Sleeping Too Much: Ferrets sleep a lot. They also tend to sleep in the most uncomfortable positions, but it is the most comfortable position ever to your ferret! Some sleep so soundly that their owners think they are dead.

Snoring: Some ferrets snore when they sleep, and it sounds just like they are breathing hard.

Toileting: Ferrets usually will need to toilet after they have awakened from a nap. If you are just litter training your new ferret, place him in the litter box every time he wakes up. If he hops out, just place him back in.

Yawning/Stretching: When ferrets wake up, they seem to yawn and stretch a lot. This is very common, so don't worry if your ferret does this excessively.

some just don't catch on as well, while others do considerably better. At least ferrets are small, so their accidents are pretty easy to clean up. Finally, if your ferret seems to have completely forgotten all about litter boxes, you might need to retrain him by confining him to a smaller area or even a cage for a week or so. Gradually expand his space as he catches on again.

Problem Behaviours

Ferrets are wonderful pets. They are intelligent, loving, charming, and clever animals who are a pleasure to own. But any owner can tell you that they also can be mischievous and rambunctious at times. Being a responsible "ferret parent" means that your pet should be properly supervised at all times and that you make every effort to understand his behaviour, what it means, and deal with it appropriately.

Quite often, if you take time to know your ferret, you will realise that he may be misbehaving because something is amiss in his world. Although some behaviours are just natural instinct, others are the result of some discomfort in his environment or a medical issue. When your ferret displays problem behaviour, it usually means that he's misunderstood, unhappy, or sick.

It's your job to find out what is provoking this behaviour, to deal with it patiently, and to work on solving the problem together. Harsh punishment or correction is never the answer. The best way to avoid troubling behaviour is to deal with it before it becomes a problem. Sometimes it may be your own behaviour that needs modification. Whatever the case, any bad situation can be remedied so that the bond you share with your pet can continue to grow.

Biting

Ferrets have thick skin covered with fur. It's natural for kits to play fight with each other, not feel pain, and come out of it all without a scratch. You must teach your ferret what is and isn't acceptable behaviour.

As your ferret grows from kithood to adolescence, he will eventually outgrow the nipping behaviour. Into adulthood and throughout his life, he may, on occasion, still nip for attention, a treat, or to simply let you know

who's the boss. As you play with him, do not allow him to continually nip at your ankles (one of their favourite places), your hands, or anywhere else. Roughhousing and allowing your pet to do so only encourages him to nip you even harder.

Never flick or hit a ferret (or any pet) for nipping. It will only make the ferret nervous or angry, and he may then bite out of fear. If a child sees you yelling at or hitting an animal, she undoubtedly will repeat this abusive behaviour, possibly creating a bite situation. Violence breeds violence!

The most effective way to respond to a nip is to gently grasp the ferret by the scruff of the neck, calmly remove him, then look into his eyes and say "No!" Then quickly divert his attention elsewhere, such as by playing with a toy. This is a natural, nonpainful form of positive punishment. You may have to repeat this several times until your ferret learns who the pack leader is. It is up to you to teach your pet acceptable behaviour. Ferrets have

Ferrets

Proper Pet Handling

While it is true that young children can learn many lessons from animals, it is also true that animals need to be cared for by responsible adults and children. Youngsters need to be taught that pets are not stuffed toys and must be handled with care. Instruct them to follow these safety guidelines:

- Don't go near any pet or open up his cage without an adult around.
- Don't move quickly toward animals or go near them if they are fighting.
- Don't wake up a sleeping pet.
- Don't kick, hit, or bite a pet or scream in his ear.
- Don't tease or chase a pet around the house.
- Don't put your face next to a pet's face.
- Don't poke fingers in a pet's eyes; pull on his tail, ears, or fur; pick him up by the tail; or step on him.
- Don't poke fingers in a pet's cage.
- Don't feed a pet any treats unless the owner gives permission.
- Don't eat the pet's food.
- Don't put fingers in your mouth after handling or cleaning up after a pet, and always wash hands after doing so.

no idea their playful nipping is hurting you. They will need to learn that playful nipping is only acceptable with animal companions.

You also can try giving a misbehaving ferret a time-out by confining him to his cage and ignoring him for a few minutes, which can be very effective, especially if there's another ferret wandering around conspicuously having fun. You can also cover your hands with a bitter apple spray or the paste so that nipping tastes bad.

Patience, repetition, and motivation are the keys to successful training.

Chewing

Ferrets are not chewers like rabbits and other rodents, so you shouldn't have many problems with ferrets chewing on wires or cables. However, rubber is a ferret favourite and so should be avoided, especially rubber bands. Ferrets do tend to chew up some toys, so you need to be observant that they don't ingest items that will require surgery to remove. Keeping vinyl and rubber objects away from your ferret completely is your best course of action.

Limiting your ferret's access to dangerous chewing options and giving him suitable items with which to entertain himself will keep him out of trouble. Making sure that he has plenty of safe toys to play with will help to protect the items in your home that you don't want to become damaged.

Digging

Ferrets love to dig, and they come by it naturally. Your ferret's ancestors were burrowing animals who dug their nests deep into the ground. Normal targets for digging include cage corners, litter boxes, potted plants, and carpeting. You should give your ferret suitable places to dig, like a dig box. (See Chapter 2 for appropriate dig box choices.)

While you won't be able to prevent your ferret from digging, you can do some things to prevent him from damaging your personal property. Keep your plants up high, or cover the soil with wire, large decorative rocks, or tin foil. For carpeting, try using plastic carpet runners. Many people find these invaluable to the preservation of their carpeting. Others simply remove the carpeting where their ferret will be playing. Tile or vinyl flooring is much easier to clean, too.

Finding the Lost Ferret

Ferrets love to explore and hide. Because they are quite curious and mischievous, they will take any opportunity to slip out of the house. And who hasn't on occasion left an outside door open accidentally? If your ferret suddenly disappeared, would you know what to do?

If you can't find your ferret, immediately search the entire house to make sure that he isn't nestled or hiding somewhere indoors. Call your ferret's name or squeeze his favourite squeaky toy. If he is sleeping, the noise of the toy will normally wake him up. If you cannot find your ferret in the house, check all around outside. Look in the garage and in sheds; check bushes; and look inside cars (including under the bonnet). Place a cage outside your home. Put food and water along with your ferret's favourite blanket and toy inside—this may lure him out of hiding.

Next, speak to your neighbours and ask them to be on the lookout. Show them a recent photo of your pet if you can because they may not know what a ferret is or what one looks like. (Ferrets are often mistaken for minks or rats, and sometimes they are chased, beaten with brooms, or even shot at.) Ask permission to check your neighbours' sheds, garages, and, possibly dryer vents.

Your ferret's natural curiosity could lead him to sneak outdoors. Constant supervision is a must.

With a little time and effort, your charming but mischievous ferret will become a treasured family member for years to come.

Place notices with a photo of your ferret along with your contact information on street corners in your neighbourhood, at grocery shops, and at petrol stations. Put an ad in the local newspaper. Offer a reward. Also, call your local ferret club, veterinary surgeries, rescue centre, and wildlife centre to report your ferret missing. Give them a description along with your contact information. Remember to call back frequently.

It is usually a good idea to let your neighbours know that you have a ferret and what he looks like *before* something happens. If your pet should sneak out and go next door, your neighbours will know to call you. The best way to prevent an escape is constant supervision while your ferret is out of his cage. Failing to know where he is at all times is a recipe for disaster.

The Good Life

When sharing your home, having a happy, well-adjusted pet can make all the difference. Taking the time to understand your ferret and all of his behaviours and needs will not only guarantee a harmonious household but will build the trust and relationship you share over the many years you will spend together.

Resources

Clubs and Societies

The British Ferret Club
www.britishferretclub.co.uk
E-mail: PROfficer@britishferretclub.co.uk
E-mail: secretary@britishferretclub.co.uk

Scottish Ferret Club
www.fishnferrets.pwp.blueyonder.co.uk/ScottishFerrets

All Shires Ferret Club
www.allshiresferretclub.co.uk

Ashfield Ferret Club
www.ashfieldferretclub.com

Wessex Ferret Club
PO Box 6142, Christchurch
Dorset, BH23 9AU
www.wessexferretclub.co.uk

Hants & Berks Ferret Club
www.hbferretclub.co.uk

North Bucks Ferret Club
www.northbucksferretclub.org.uk

Ferrets

Veterinary and Health Resources

British Veterinary Association (BVA)
7 Mansfield Street
London
W1G 9NQ
Telephone: 020 7636 6541
Fax: 020 7436 2970
E-mail: bvahq@bva.co.uk
www.bva.co.uk

British Small Animal Veterinary Association (BSAVA)
Woodrow House
1 Telford Way
Waterwells Business Park
Quedgley
Gloucester GL2 2AB
Telephone: 01452 726700
email: customerservices@bsava.com
www.bsava.com

British Association of Homeopathic Veterinary Surgeons
Alternative Veterinary Medicine Centre
Chinham House
Stanford in the Vale
Oxfordshire
SN7 8NQ
Email: enquiries@bahvs.com
www.bahvs.com

British Veterinary Hospitals Association (BHVA)
Station Bungalow
Main Road, Stockfield
Northumberland NE43 7HJ
Telephone: 07966 901619
Email: office@bvha.org.uk
www.BVHA.org.uk

Animal Welfare and Rescue Organisations

Royal Society for the Prevention of Cruelty to Animals (RSPCA)
Telephone: 0870 3335 999
Fax: 0870 7530 284
www.rspca.org.uk

Scottish Society for the Prevention of Cruelty to Animals (SSPCA)
Braehead Mains
603 Queensferry Road
Edinburgh EH4 6EA
Telephone: 0131 339 0222

British Veterinary Association Animal Welfare Foundation (BVA AWF) 7 Mansfield Street
London W1G 9NQ
Telephone: 0207 636 6541
Email: bva-awf@bva.co.uk
www.bva-awf.org.uk

Pet Rescue UK
www.pet-rescue.org.uk

British Federation of Ferret Welfares
www.bffw.btik.com

Chapel Lane Ferret Welfare (West Midlands)
www.chapel-lane.net

Chase Ferret Rescue (Staffordshire)
www.freewebs.com/chaseferretrescue/index.htm

Droitwich Feffet Welfare
(Worcestershire)
www.droitwichferretwelfare.co.uk

The Ferret Hotel & Rescue
(Nottingham)
www.ashfieldferrets.co.uk

The Ferret Sanctuary (Epsom)
www.ferretinfo.org

The Ferret Sanctuary (Worthing)
www.ferretfascination.co.uk

Fuzzy Ferret Rescue (Nottinghamshire)
http://beehive.thisisnottingham.co.uk/fuzzyferretrescue

Fife Ferret Rescue (Fife)
www.fifeferretrescue.co.uk

Hull & East Riding Ferret Rescue
http://beehive.thisishull.co.uk/ferretrescue

Mercie Ferret Welfare & Rescue
(Coventry)
www.mercia41.freeserve.co.uk

South Staffs Ferret Rescue
www.southstaffsferrets.co.uk

South West Ferred Rescue (Camborne)
www.southstaffsferrets.co.uk

Tayside Ferret Rescue (Tayside North of Scotland & Fife)
www.taysideferretrescue.btik.com

Resources

Websites

The following websites contain information on all aspects of ferret care and links to other informative websites.

All About Pets
www.allaboutpets.org.uk
The Blue Cross site provides information on pet care and husbandry for all household pets.

PDSA
www.pdsa.org.uk
The PDSA website provides in-depth information on all aspects of pet care, health, first aid and veterinary care advice.

Pets World
www.petsworld.co.uk
These informative pages provide advice on housing, feeding and general care of your gerbil.

Ferret Education & Research Trust (FERT)
Holm Park,
Office 231, 27 Colmore Row
Birmingham, B3 2EW
Telephone: 0870 8031475
E-mail: info@ferrettrust.org
www.ferrettrust.org

Pet-Sitting Services

The National Association of Professional Pet Sitters
17000 Commerce Parkway
Suite C
Mt. Laurel, NJ 08054
Phone: (856) 439-0324
E-mail: napps@ahint.com

Pet Sitters International
201 East King Street
King, NC 27021
Phone: (336) 983-9222
E-mail: info@petsit.com
Website: www.petsit.com

Publications

Magazines

Fur and Feather Magazine
Printing for Pleasure Ltd
Elder House, Chattisham
Ipswich, Suffolk, IP8 3QE
Telephone: 01473 652789
E-mail: info@furandfeather.co.uk

Online Pet Magazine
www.petmag.co.uk

Ferrets First Magazine (online)
www.ferretsfirst.net
E-mail: ferretsfirst@btopenworld.com

Books

Land, Bobbye. *Your Outta Control Ferret*. New Jersey: TFH Publications, Inc., 2003.

Horton-Bussey, Claire, *101 Facts About Ferrets*, Interpet Publishing, 2001

Morton, E Lynn, *Ferrets (A Complete Pet Owner's Manual)*, Barron's Educational Series, Inc.

Bucsis, Gerry & Somerville, Barbara, The Ferret Handbook, Barron's Educational Series, Inc.

Dustman, Karen, *Ferrets (Complete Care Made Easy)*, BowTie Press

106

Index

Note: Boldfaced numbers indicate illustrations.

Index